MW00862248

FIXING TO MAKE A FORTUNE

Mr. Rehab's Guide to the World
of Renovating Houses

by

Pete Youngs

Copyright © 2020 by Pete Youngs

All rights reserved.

Printed in the United States of America. No part of this book may be used or reproduced in any manner whatsoever without written permission except in the case by brief quotations, articles and reviews.

DISCLAIMER & LIMIT OF LIABILITY: The teachings, practices, activities, techniques, examples, ideas, principles, and methods in this book are only personal observations based on my own experiences in the field and should not be used in conflict with any local restrictions or laws, nor should they replace the advice of licensed professionals.

Published by Pete Youngs

FIRST EDITION

ISBN: 978-0-578-23242-3

TABLE OF CONTENTS

ACKNOWLEDGEMENTS 1

INTRODUCTION 3

A COMMON ISSUE FACING REHAB INVESTORS.................................. 5

AFTER THE STORM... 7

ALWAYS BE ON THE LOOKOUT FOR PROPERTY................................ 11

ASK THE EXPERTS... 15

BUYING WITH PRIVATE MONEY 17

COMMON MISTAKES TO AVOID 19

CREATING WEALTH REHABBING PROPERTY..................................... 21

DEALING WITH MOLD.. 25

DO IT YOURSELF ADVICE... 29

DOES DOOR KNOCKING WORK IN TODAY'S MARKET?..................... 33

DON'T GET SCAMMED BY CONTRACTORS 35

ESTIMATING REHAB COSTS IN TODAY'S MARKET 39

GIVING OLD KITCHENS AND BATHROOM AN INEXPENSIVE FACELIFT 41

HIRING A CONTRACTOR 45

INEXPENSIVE REPAIRS WITH "BONDO" 49

IT DEPENDS ON THE WEATHER 51

MAKING HUGE PROFITS WITH MOLD INSPECTION 53

OUTLINE FOR A BASIC HOME RENOVATION 57

PAINTING OVER WALLPAPER 59

THE POWER OF TWO... 61

PROSPECTUS FOR PRIVATE MONEY LOANS 65

PUT THOUSANDS OF DOLLARS OF PROFIT IN YOUR POCKET
WITHOUT DOING THE WORK YOURSELF!......................................67

QUICK, INEXPENSIVE ROOF REPAIRS 69

REAL ESTATE CRUISES, MY FAVORITE NETWORKING 71

RELATIONSHIPS THAT BUILD WEALTH..............................75

THE REMODELING CONTRACT..............................81

THE SCOPE OF WORK (Don't get an estimate without one!) 85

SEAL THE DEAL WITH BEAUTIFUL CURB APPEAL 89

SEVEN QUESTIONS TO ASK CONTRACTORS....................................93

SPRING FLINGS FOR YOUR PROPERTIES I 95

SPRING FLINGS FOR YOUR PROPERTIES II 99

SPRING FLINGS FOR YOUR PROPERTIES III 101

SWAT – SECRET WAYS AND TECHNIQUES 105

TERMITES CAN EAT YOUR HOUSE, AND YOUR PROFITS...............109

THEFT PROOF REHABBING..113

THINGS THAT MAKE YOU GO HMMM!..........................117

TIPS TO SELL HOUSES FAST....................................121

TOP 10 RENOVATIONS TO ADD VALUE.........................125

TOXIC TERRORS THAT AFFECT HOMES 129

WINTERIZING YOUR HOME 133

INCLUDED IN THE SWAT SYSTEM 135

HAVE PETE YOUNGS AT YOUR LOCAL REIA OR CONVENTION.............136

RECOMMENDED RESOURCES 139

ACKNOWLEDGEMENTS

I would like to give special thanks to the people who have been a part of my life and made an influence. I can't name them all but let's start here.

My parents Alan and Hilda Youngs. The things I have learned from you have been with me all my life and you will be in my heart forever. Rest in peace brother Paul, you are missed.

My wife Barbara and son James, I am so grateful to have shared all we have together. Barb You are the reason I am who I am.

My daughter in law Jessica and grandsons Nolan and Remington. The joy you bring to me is amazing.

Sister Suzanne Freeman and Bill Freeman, we have shared the best of times and you are priceless to me.

Jeff Hedge, Anna, Owen and Lily. You are a gift from GOD.

Julie, Jordan and Joey Freeman have been so fun watching you all turn to successful adults. P H D P F S if ya know what I mean.

Tony Youngs, Liz and Grace. Best real estate trainer by far. Partners for years, bros forever. You got me into real estate. Thanks for everything.

Carl Fischer, Vicki Fischer for being friends before business partners. Let's continue to travel the world together as usual.

Mike Butler and Beth Butler. Friends and mentors always!

Larry Goins, Pam Goins. Friends forever, love you both.

Kandas Broome, Matt Broome. Ya'll are the best. Thank You.

INTRODUCTION

I have been a general contractor/investor for over thirty years. As a leading expert in my field, I've written many in-depth articles and collected a wealth of information and helpful tips covering just about everything you might want to know about home renovation and rehabbing.

I'm very pleased to now share my knowledge and collected articles in this book.

Happy Rehabbing!

Pete Youngs
Aka Mr. Rehab

A COMMON ISSUE FACING REHAB INVESTORS

I have been doing rehabs and investing for almost 30 years now. Along the way I have learned literally thousands of money saving techniques that I share with investors nationwide in my Rehab 101 system and training events. Some of the most common mistakes new investors and seasoned alike, can be avoided by knowing just a few things before you get started. In the following, you will find some valuable items that will save you a lot of pain and grief as well as a lot of money.

Many people are at the mercy of sellers and what they disclose (or don't) when they buy a fixer property. One of the most common mistakes people make, is assuming that they know what has been done to the property before they bought it. An easy part that is often overlooked on a property is how was the property painted before. Seems like a minor concern until you look at the serious side.

You cannot paint latex paint over oil-based paint. Most fixer fans love to use latex paints. They are easier to work with and clean up with soap and water is a breeze. Most also assume that everyone before them has painted with the easier latex paint. Many problems can occur if you put latex on top of oil based paint.

First off. The latex paint will seem to have a hard time covering the oil paint. It may seem to smear a bit, instead of flow evenly. The other problem is that even though it looks like you paint is covering properly, it actually is like putting water on butter. It just simply will not stick!!

This is going to cause any surface painted to flake and chip. The most common areas that this is a factor will be on the doors; windows and wood trim in the home. Literally hundreds of times in a house, someone has painted the surfaces with some cheap paint just to give a cosmetic face-lift to the property. Now, and until this problem has been corrected, it will be a maintenance nightmare constantly requiring touch up and repaints due to the easy flaking areas that will scratch and peel anytime they are bumped or grazed by everyday living.

The first step is to make sure that you are not the person who paints the latex over the oil paint to start the problem. A couple of ways to prevent this is before you ever paint a surface, test it!! You can get a product called (Goof Off) or you can use a canned product called (xylene) to test paint before you apply any coating. Both can be found in the paint dept of most hardware stores and will run you about $5.00 to buy. Testing is the same for both products. Step one is to get a white cloth and pour some of the solvent (either of the two I listed) and rub the cloth on the surface you are testing with medium scrub strength. If the paint comes off on to the rag (actually melting the paint and removing it) then the paint is a latex paint and can be painted over again with latex, and no other prep is required. If you appear to only clean the surface and no paint residue comes off on the rag, this means the paint is oil based. Here you have 2 choices. You can paint it again with oil-based paint with no other prep needed, or you can do what I prefer. I will paint the surface with an oil-based primer such as (Kilz brand). After the oil primer dries, I can now recoat with a latex paint. Now and forever more I can paint with the latex paints, because I will be painting latex over latex.

So there is no confusion, a latex paint will not stick to oil based paint, however, latex paint will stick to oil based primer. That way you have converted the area back to using the easy latex paint.

So what about if you have a property that someone before has painted the latex over oil and left you with the problem of fixing the flaking paint. The solution is to follow the steps above for painting over oil…Use the Kilz primer and then paint with latex afterwards.

I recommend that if the flaking is occurring that you also use a paint additive called (EMULSA-BOND). This is a product found in paint and hardware stores. It causes latex paint to adhere to surfaces that are flaking or chalky. I hope this will help you from making a costly mistake in the future.

AFTER THE STORM

After any major storm many people are faced with what to do next. I searched the internet and several agencies for answers to this question and have come up with some suggestions to help the victims of a devastating storm. First off, my prayers go out for all victims of hurricanes and storms of all types.

Most times an area will be out of power for up to two to four weeks or even more. Using generators in well ventilated areas may be a way to temporarily restore some power for much needed items such as repair tools and cooking and heating food and such. Get a radio and listen to get news of help and other instructions. It will warn of dangers and tell you where to get help.

You will need to carry some sort of ID at all times so police and other authorities can know if you should be in the area. Many looters and such are now going to be in the area with less than good intentions and the police can normally tell if someone has a need to be in the area. Also, avoid driving if possible or if your car is mobile. With all the debris and downed electric wires, you could be putting yourself at risk by driving. There is also a chance the officials may not let you back in an area once you leave for several days.

Open all your doors and windows to start the drying process from your house. It is important to remove water as it will develop bacteria and mold and really put you at risk for illness. Do not use matches or flame, candles and such until you are sure that no gas lines have been ruptured. Cover the roof if damaged and start to make small fast repairs to avoid more damage to your home.

Food and water will be scarce. The radio will tell you of efforts to get these to you. If you have anything salvageable to use, make sure it is canned goods and nonperishable. Any water that you use should be boiled for 10 minutes before use and you really need water from other areas if possible.

Since all water that may surround your house will be contaminated, use any safety precautions you can to avoid contact with germs and bacteria such as gloves, glasses and shoes if you can. When you can get out to get materials, you want disinfectants such as Microban or shockwave for mold and mildew. Odoban is a good cleaner and disinfectant and cleaning anything you may be able to keep is worth the effort.

If you must leave your home, secure it as best as you can. Unfortunately, some people will loot and take what little you may have left as they are desperate. As time goes by, you will need to start making contacts with the people who can help. Make a sign of who your insurance is and put it up in clear view of your house. When you can start making phone calls for assistance from insurance companies, the Red Cross and FEMA. Find out if you have flood damage insurance and what other coverage you may have. If all is lost, contact anyplace that may have your info.

Start keeping receipts for reimbursement for living expenses and repairs as you do them. Bills for anything related to the storm may possibly be paid back to you. If you can salvage any before pictures of your home and belongings, keep these for reimbursement. If they have been destroyed, contact friends and relatives that may have pictures that may help. Even Christmas or birthday pics may contain images of reimbursable items. Anything may help. Also take many pictures of your damage and losses to show to insurance adjusters when that point arises.

When you get a visit from an adjuster, do not settle totally all at once. You may incur damage or loss from things that happen later or as more time goes by. Your insurance adjuster is at no cost to you. You may be approached or seek a public adjuster to speed things up. Keep in mind that a public adjuster could charge you up to 15% of your money recovered for their services, so know up front what you are getting.

You want to comprise a list of your loss, not only real estate but also your family's personal belongings. Jewelry, tv, stereo, cars, china, guns, cars outdoor furniture and antiques. Take time to be as detailed as you can. Once you have settled it may be hard or even impossible to get any more relief. Try not to throw away damaged items of high value before being damaged. The adjuster may want to see high dollar items if they can.

Contractors may come to you in your time of need. Be careful. You as well as they know you need results fast, but all too often, scammers hit the scene. Do not pull permits for your contractor. Have them do it under these conditions. This may weed out someone who might not want to go by the rules and could stop a scam contractor from getting you while you are down.

Get all bids in writing and be very detailed about how much and what kind of material is to be used. This will be a plus when dealing with adjusters and such. Also, if your adjuster is a public adjuster, the 15% fee I mentioned earlier is not covered by your insurance. It comes out of your pocket.

From the internet, I found some numbers to call for assistance and will list them for you here. I trust that these numbers are working and valid at this time. My prayers for victims will continue and I hope that this article will help anyone in need.

TO FIND FAMILY CALL THE RED CROSS, A CHAPTER OUTSIDE THE DISASTER AREA IS THE BEST BET TO CALL ON THIS MATTER.

NATIONAL FLOOD INSURANCE 1-800-CALL-FLOOD EXT. 445

HOUSING ASSISTANCE (FEMA) 1-800-462-9029

LOST JOB...DISASTER UNEMPLOYMENT ASSISTANCE 1-800-462-9029

LEGAL HELP...DISASTER RECOVERY CENTER 1-800-525-0321

ALWAYS BE ON THE LOOKOUT FOR PROPERTY

Full time real estate investors are always looking at any and all possibilities no matter where they go. The same should be taught to beginners. Keep in mind that you will never go anywhere in the world that real estate is not the biggest product for investment you see. Done properly, every trip you take is a potential deal waiting to happen.

On one of our cruise voyages with Carl and Vicky Fischer we as always, looked at properties. With all the newest ways you can profit from real property and the fact that we are associated with many real estate investment groups nationwide, our buyer base is literally unlimited. Even if it is not something you would want to do personally, make sure you don't pass up money making situations.

We know people and groups that love the idea of AirBnB as this is a world- wide opportunity. During the cruise we went to Oahu and Maui in Hawaii. Wouldn't it be great to own a place in paradise to rent out when you were not using it? But think about this. I don't always have to be the prime investor. Maybe it is not your dream to have property in Hawaii. But to a lot of people this would be very appealing and profitable. So at one of our stops to eat lunch at a place recommended to us, we found that it was part hotel and part condo's. So after our meal, we inquired with the sales department about 1, 2, and 3 bedroom units. We gathered some written materials on price and layout and definitely the views from each of the sizes available. Then the next step would be getting comparable sales, days on market and a background of what the rise or decline of sales prices have been over the past year or two. Now even if it doesn't appeal to us, we have a network of buyers to pass this info onto and treat it as a possible Wholesale deal that we can profit by selling the contract to an interested investor.

Yes it's true, you don't always need to be the end buyer, make yourself have multiple income streams by being the bird dog too! Keep in mind that the extra time it took to check out the condo's where we had lunch anyway only took about 30 extra minutes. Even if we don't profit from a deal, we at least have the ability to possibly take the trip, lunch cost and such as a tax or business expense. How would you like to lower you travel costs considerably by using common investment strategies that qualify to be deducted from expenses and taxes? Your real estate attorney can quickly fill you in on what you can and can't do.

Our next stop was in a group of islands in Fiji. Fiji is beautiful and I always think of Tony Robbins and his motivational expertise as this area to me has a memory of trainings here. While on an excursion from the cruise ship, we by-passed the on board vendors and chose to hire our own private van and driver to take us to where we wanted to go. I have found that when I get a tour from the boat, we end up somehow at tourist sales traps during our outings and many times have found out that the driver received a cash kick back before leaving (I saw this } for bringing the group there. I also have been told by independent drivers that most of the time the contract drivers are related by family to some of the "STORES" that we stopped at.

As we headed to some of our requested places we wanted to see, our driver told us of a place that had been damaged by a storm but since it was not a boat sponsored location, it was slowly rebuilding itself back to the local favorite it once was. You see, boat sponsored places receive help and money fast to get them back to perfect so the boats can resume making money from the excursion. The place we went to had no such help. So the theme for the place we went was there were small to giant sea turtles that you could feed from the shore as well as enter the lagoon and swim with them. It was a very nice area but you could easily tell that it was damaged from strong winds. It also had some huts that were used for offering a full BBQ buffet as part of the experience. There were three buffet huts but only one open. Then we saw the area had several shower huts and bathrooms along the 100 foot wide lagoon, but only one buffet hut was open. A little further walk and also a part of the experience, there were several variety of sharks swimming in a protected area the visitors were allowed to feed. This was exiting feeding, filming and watching the sharks up close. We talked to the locals working there and got a lot of background info from them about the area.

As I have been trying to point out, real estate deals pop up everywhere without warning. You never know when an opportunity will open when you least expect it. None of us paid much attention as we first entered the lengthy dirt road leading to the venue, but there was a for sale sign just outside three or four mediocre houses shrouded with line strung laundry about a quarter mile before we arrived. As it turns out, the ones selling the houses were also the ones who owned the property that operated the venue for the turtles and sharks experience. The storm had knocked down the other for sale signs showing that the whole venue was for sale as the owners did not have the means or contacts to rebuild. They got the place going just enough to make food and bills but were overwhelmed with the longer term of fixing the place back up. Now their option was to sell it all!

Obviously sirens and light bulbs were going off in our heads to figure out exactly what did these people need in order for there to be a winning situation for seller and buyer both. Investor mode had kicked in and ideas started running through our heads. So we now know to get a plat of the land to see just how much there was. There was at least 100 acres or more potential. Now we need to find out if you can own property outright or do you pay and amount, pay the taxes on schedule, and see if you only can have a 99- year lease or what requirements does this property have.

Now keep in mind that there are so many ways this can be investigated into for different uses. Would this be something that investors just fix the venue and use it for a wildlife attraction? Most people don't automatically think this, but is it something you get under contract to offer to sell to Huge hotel chains to make a resort as it is gorgeous and a tropical paradise on many acres? Do you get interested people to come in and build luxury houses or a subdivision? Hotels, Condo's, Restaurants, shopping, retail, mixed use??? Do you think that the distressed owners would see the win for both sides if they walked away from a tough situation with a life changing amount of money that would take care of their families for the rest of their lives?

Now let me ask you this…Have I changed even just a little bit, how you may look at things the next trip you go on? Do you see that opportunity is everywhere and most people walk or drive right passed it never knowing your life could be changed in a glance of a hidden sign on a tree? Remember, this was a chance sighting based on the fact that we decided not to do a cruise ship offered excursion and went with hiring a lower cost local to take us to places that are real exotic places and not tourist traps? I am writing this as we are still doing our due diligence but I will definitely keep anyone updated who follows my writings and real estate techniques. Though my primary expertise has always been in the fix and flip scenario, I have over 3 decades of real estate experience and it just keeps growing. Never stop learning and always keep an open mind.

ASK THE EXPERTS

Q: How can I estimate house damages?

A: That is a tough question to answer, as not all repair costs are equal all over the country. What I do is get the national average cost of the repair and work it from there. At your local large hardware chain store, you can get average prices in national construction cost guidelines manuals. These are similar to car collision repair manuals. If you take a wrecked car in for an estimate, after they look at the damage, they open up a book that tells them how many man-hours and material costs are related to that type of damage, then give you a price. Doing this with home repairs will give you the same results, how many man hours, at what rate per hour, and material costs, leaving you with the total repair estimate.

Also, when getting estimates for your investment properties or your own home you should follow what I tell everyone…Most estimates come with brief descriptions and a total price at the bottom. Keep in mind that almost any repair can be broken down into one of three things. That would be the square foot, the linear foot or the square yard. Square feet covers things like building living use area, decks, fences and painting inside and out. Linear feet would include gutters, downspouts, wood trim, baseboards, soffit and fascia and more. Square yards would be for carpeting and most flooring as well as pouring concrete slabs and driveways. Get your estimates broken down to one of these common units (per foot cost) and call local suppliers to see if you are being charged more than the average per foot price in your region.

Q: I have zero experience in construction. Should I take a class?

A: Definitely yes. I teach classes all over the U.S. weekly and love getting the e mails and letters from people who have attended and used the things learned to save money as well as be really involved in the process of buying, fixing and selling properties.

Education in the real estate business is the best thing you can do. This is one of the few times where you can never really know too much. I would also want you to join your local real estate investment club. Right now today, if not sooner. You will be well rewarded for joining based on the fact that you have more resources there than in any one place at any given time. You have the experience of the people running the club every month, as well as their advice and expertise. Your club may even be run by world class experts such as FLREIA. You have access monthly to hard money lenders, networking, a place to buy and a place to sell. Last but not least, they bring in people to educate you and provide training classes, seminars and bootcamps to further you in your quest.

Q: What kind of capital do I need before I buy a home to rehab and sell?

A: There are still ways to buy distressed properties as well as others with no money down techniques. You can also buy from wholesalers, people who buy and sell the contracts to other investors and most wholesalers are themselves or connected to hard money lenders who can put you in a deal supplying the house, the rehab money included in the purchase, and still have good profits in the resale of your deal. Many people have started out like that who felt the need not to use their own credit or money for whatever reasons. There really (to me) is not a set amount to have, but I do know that most people should have enough capital to cover the estimated repairs that you have been quoted, plus about six months holding costs. Holding costs would be any payments, monthly or otherwise, that you have agreed to pay (such as a mortgage payment in some types of deals). It does not always need to be held that long, but it is a safe cushion on a majority of deals.

BUYING WITH PRIVATE MONEY

When buying a property, sometimes it is better to use other people's money (OPM) than your own. This is how a lot of investors get their start. There are several different ways to do this, but the most common two are Hard money Loans or Private Money Loans.

When using a hard money lender, you may have to pay points up front to get the loan, then a percentage rate of interest only payments until the property is sold or the term of the loan has been met. A typical example of this would be as follows. Using round figures, let's say you borrowed $100,000 at 5 points and 13% interest for 1 year. You would have paid $5000 up front (5 points) and then 13% interest only payments until paid off. There is normally no pre-payment penalty for early payoff. Also, the lender will typically only loan 65 to 70% of the (LTV)Loan to value of the property to insure the money in case loan defaults. The lender will loan based on after repair value (ARV).

Private money loans are also based on about 65 to 70% of the properties ARV and unless specified otherwise go for 12 months or less. These loans in my opinion are easier to get because more people can do private money than are in the business of hard money. Both hard and private money will secure a lien on the subject property to guarantee payment. When I said private money may be easier, let me clarify why, and again this is my opinion.

Hard money lenders are "In The Business" of loaning money and do it as a major income stream, therefore charge points. A private money lender may do this less frequently and therefore charges a flat interest rate without points. Private money can be a person loaning money from a Self-Directed IRA or 401k and do it for tax free or tax differed return on their investment.

(See www.CamaPlan.com for free webinars and info) on such things. Private money may use a flat rate too, commonly being about 10%

interest only. This can build wealth quickly and at much higher dollar amounts than just your annual allowance. If someone is making ½ to 1% interest on their money, then the opportunity to make 10% and being secured by the property is a very appealing prospect. Private money may also come from other sources such as friends, relatives and business acquaintances. Rules for using self directed IRA and 401k funds are different than friends and relatives but are readily available all over the country. Camaplan as listed above is my favorite source for rules and requirements, and again has free training.

As far as information on using a hard money lenders, my suggestion is to join your local real estate investment club, (also known as a REIA) real estate investors association. They are the best source for new and seasoned investors alike and offer education as well as reliable contacts for Hard money loans, mortgages, insurance, buyers, sellers, contractors and basically everything an investor on any level would need. With that being said, let me also add this too, and like I said before this is my opinion.

When choosing a REIA (real estate investor association) I suggest that you Choose one that is a member of the National Real Estate Investors Association (nationalreia.org). This is a nationwide governing body of investment clubs all over the country. They make sure that all Clubs meet strict ethical and moral standards and make sure that you are dealing with the best investor associations out there. I have been a personal supporter and member for over 30 years and attend their Investor Cruises (what a blast while getting educated) as well as the mid year conferences to share new ideas and such. They also provide nationwide benefits and discounts nationwide with such sponsors as Home Depot, Sherwin Williams and countless others. Please research www.nationalreia.org for more information.

Here are a few, but not all of requirements that need to be met to be considered for hard or private money loans nationwide.

COMMON MISTAKES TO AVOID

Beginners and seasoned investors alike are prone to making mistakes. Most mistakes can be easily avoided by just listening to people talking at your local REIA group or meet up sessions.

Some mistakes are minor and have little impact on the end result of selling or renting your property when others can become nightmares. This will not be the only portion I write on mistake but this one I am sure will affect everyone somehow.

One of the most guaranteed things you will have to do in your own house or investment property is painting. If you do it yourself or hire it out, you MUST know and follow this advice. You cannot paint latex paint over oil-based paint anytime. It will peel and flake badly within about 3 to six months. Also, the paint will easily chip and scrape off as latex paint does not adhere to oil-based paint. You can however paint latex paint over an oil-based primer. I always use oil-based primer and sealer in one, such as KILZ or ZINZER. This will prime, seal in any stains and can be painted over with any latex paint.

To know what type of paint you are painting over, there are a few ways to test the surfaces and paint over it correctly. You all may have heard of Goof Off, a canned liquid whose claim is that it removes dried latex paint. This costs about $5 in hardware stores for about 4 ounces. Squirt this on a white rag and lightly scrub an area on walls, trim, windows, doors and gutters or whatever you are going to paint. If it melts the paint on to the rag, it's latex paint and you can easily just paint over it with latex, no problem. If all it does is clean the surface and no paint melts onto the rag, it is oil-based paint and must be painted with oil again.

There is another way to avoid having to paint the oil-based paint. If you use an oil-based primer/sealer (KILZ) to prime the previously painted surfaces, you can paint latex on top of the oil-based primer and from here to eternity you can just paint latex on you house. That is how you change an oil painted house to being the easier latex painted house forever. You may also use XYLENE or DENATURED ALCOHOL instead of Goof Off. This will ensure that your painted surfaces resist peeling away.

Another mistake is how do it yourselfers and painters paint cabinets and paneling in properties. The finished product can show runs, drips and brush marks making the job look shoddy. To paint any stained surface, first wipe it down with white vinegar in full strength with a sponge or cloth. This will remove grease from cabinets and oils from wood stains and paneling. Then I apply one coat of Kilz oil-based primer. Before I apply the primer/sealer, I have it tinted to the same color I am painting the cabinets or paneling (usually a white color). With the white vinegar and the sealer/primer applied, I am positive that my latex paint will now stick. But here is the kicker!!! No matter what brand of paint you use (I use BEHR marquee from Home Depot) It MUST say "self leveling" latex paint. This self leveling paint is designed to dry smooth as glass and never leave brush marks or runs on the surface. Most people even pro painters, do not use my vinegar, sealer/primer and self leveling paint techniques and end up with cabinets that have runs drips and brush marks and paneling that will lets stains seep through within a short time after painting and will certainly look bad and need repainting.

I have hundreds more techniques to share that will stop costly mistakes and I plan on writing about them all.

CREATING WEALTH REHABBING PROPERTY

When I was growing up and about to graduate, I wondered what path to take as I entered the life of leaving mom and dad's house and making it on my own. It was always a dream of mine, like everyone to become wealthy and be my own boss. So in my last year in high school, I got into a work for credit program that allowed me to get out of school early and go to work for school credit. I was given a job painting the inside of vacant properties at an apartment complex for a general contracting company. Like all jobs, I started at the bottom of the scale and was a trim man (painting the doors, windows and baseboards with a brush) following behind a spray man. He was a higher paid person and basically ran our crew for the G.C.

This is when my entrepreneur spirit was born. I quickly made friends with this spray man and he eagerly taught me how to paint with an airless paint sprayer. I was then given a raise from $5.00 per hour to $7.00 and they set me up with my own crew. It was here that I started to learn the pricing structure, the estimating techniques and how and where to get deals on materials and cheaper labor. Within a year or so, I started my own painting and remodeling company and began getting contracts to paint and remodel houses and apartments. I found that I was really making quite a bit of money, and little did I know at the time that I was setting a lifelong path of making money through rehabbing properties.

After a few more years in the business, I started to get big commercial jobs like Fidelity National Banks, Publix Distribution Center, MCI, part of the 1996 Atlanta Games etc.

It had become that I no longer could be physically working on the job, I now had to be the general contractor and oversee all aspects of the job myself. My finding was that a general contractor got the contracts, ran the job and labor, handled the materials and pocketed as much as 50% of the money charged for the job. The rest he paid out in labor and materials. What a great concept of making money! I would continue to get the jobs and hire out the labor and pocket huge dollars while other people did the work!!!

Well as I had come full circle in learning the ropes of rehabbing, my brother had bought some books and tapes at a seminar and coaxed me into fixing up the properties that he was buying. We quickly found that the real estate business and the property rehab business was a no brainer and started our real estate investing career by joining forces and a company to buy, fix up and sell properties full time.

By sending in copies of profit checks to the person whose books and tapes my brother had bought, he immediately got us involved in the business of teaching people how to buy, fix up and sell properties making huge profits all over the country. That is what started the teaching aspect of our real estate investing careers over 15 years ago. After buying almost everyone's books and tapes systems that ever came down the pike, we now had become respected teachers of the trade and for the past seven years have shared the stage with almost all of the well known authors and lecturers on seminar circuits and national conventions. Also for the past seven years we had been contracted by the big names to teach Foreclosure-Rehab Bootcamps to thousands of students nationwide. But my favorite thing that I do is speaking to real estate investment clubs. I remember being involved and listening to real people in the club that had been using the techniques and actually making money in real estate…

No matter what strategy of real estate investing you are doing, wholesale properties, foreclosures or any other, the most common place that people reduce their profits is in the fix up or rehab. Most people do not have the knowledge to estimate damage or cost of repairs. They have to depend on the contractor and hope that the costs and repairs are reasonable and can be done without taking the majority of the expected profits.

Well this is where my expertise is it's keenest. I over the past 15 years or more have developed a way to teach anyone the ins and outs of rehabbing properties for profit. It is possible to lower your rehab costs by 50% to 75% less than the going rates.

You can act as your own general contractor and oversee your own jobs. If you are handy, you will be able to save a lot of money by do it yourself techniques. If you are not, there are several ways that you can hire out subcontractors and semi skilled labor yourself for a great savings in either cash in your pocket or equity in your property. Learning how and where to get contractor discounts is a must for any investor. Being able to do simple estimating on your own proves to be a great way of comparing estimates you get from your contractors. You can save money by pulling your own permits when applicable. Even knowing what day is best to rent equipment from a tool rental yard can save you hundreds of dollars.

Learn to run every property you do by acting as your own general contractor. In most cases not only will it increase your profits thousands of dollars in profit or equity, but you can pay yourself a salary or fee to run the job also. Just remember more money is lost in the fix up of a property than most other factors. So my suggestion is to educate yourself in all aspects of the fix up of properties. It is an absolute must for seasoned or new investors alike. This can increase the profit in any property from hundreds to thousands of dollars. Every rehab technique that is a cost cutter puts cash in your pocket that would otherwise end up in someone else's. Keep it in your pocket…it's your money!

DEALING WITH MOLD

In nearly 30 years as a contractor/investor I have faced many problems with houses not only in the repairs, but also in the conditions that affect houses. One topic that has been on the rise for a few years now is mold and how it affects houses and the people in them.

Blamed for unknown illness and allergies, mold has become a hot topic when it is present on a house indoors or out. I will always pressure wash a house before I rent or sell, because this removes any visible signs of dirt and mold, and also improves the appearance of the house. Almost all pressure washers (rented or owned) have an attachment called a chemical injector. This allows for the machine to mix a solution of regular household bleach and water as it is applied to the house. The mixture kills the mold and the pressure removes the residue. This is easily done by just about anyone. It's like taking your car to the dollar car wash. The water pressure is slightly higher (2400 to 3000 psi average) and if you can wash your car, then you can wash your house. The main idea is to stay 12 inches away from the surface you are cleaning and this will not remove paint or damage materials being cleaned. You can strip flaking paint and such by getting closer than 12 inches, if you need to. Pressure washers can be rented for about $60.00 per day. I use them for cleaning the siding, roofs, decks, fences and driveways. A hydra scrub is an attachment that can make cleaning driveways much easier.

Mold on the inside of the house is a different problem. Normally caused by moisture and bad ventilation, indoor mold causes many problems with health and the general appearance of the home. Anywhere that has warm, damp conditions can cause mold to breed. This means that bathrooms, shower stalls, basements, kitchens and crawl spaces are prone to have a mold issue arise. The most common mold and mildew forms are ugly and a nuisance, but can be removed effectively by getting a spray bottle and mixing a 50/50 solution of household bleach and water. This can be sprayed directly on the mold itself and will normally kill the mold or mildew on contact. Then you can just rinse and your problem is gone. There is no real need to buy expensive specialty cleaners when this technique works just fine.

The problem though, is that this is only a temporary fix and the mold conditions will return and you will need to repeat the process. The only way to make this problem go away is to change the conditions. In the bathroom, an exhaust fan may reduce the damp conditions. For other parts of the house you may need a dehumidifier to relieve the conditions that cause fungal growth. In basements and crawl spaces, I have found sump pumps to work well. The big thing is, you must remove the damp, moist conditions to stop the growth.

Mold and mildew come in colors. Black, green and white and have a smell that resembles damp soil. A musty odor in a room could indicate a mold problem that you can't see. One of the biggest scares these days is referred to as "Black Mold". Don't fret… Just because it's black, does not mean that it is the dreaded black mold that requires remediation. Black mold has become a scary term in the real estate business due to its expensive removal. I have actually seen instances that people had been forced to move out of the residence while the black mold and the materials that it had affected were removed. If you find yourself in a position where you have a property that has been inspected and found to have the dreaded (Black Mold) that causes serious illness, here's what you might expect.

First, there has to be three sets of people involved. There is a consultant. This is the entity that confirms that you have the black mold that is dangerous. Then you have the remediation contractor. This is the contractor that removes and all items affected with the mold such as drywall, siding, wood, flooring, wallpaper and such.

Third is the general contractor. This is who comes in to replace everything that had to be removed and to get the house put back to it's pre loss condition. Keep in mind that the three must be separate entities and can not be affiliated with each other. This would cause a conflict of interest. This ordeal looks like a sci-fi movie because the people who come out to remove the affected items dress up in Haz-Mat suits (hazardous materials) and have special vacuums and tools that most are not used to seeing. This process can cause several thousands of dollars to repair.

So my advice is this. Learn to properly inspect a house for undesirable conditions yourself. If you can find defects about a house that would stop you from buying on your own, then you have saved hundreds of dollars that you would have paid someone to tell you why you shouldn't buy the house. However, if you don't find anything and you want to buy the house, then you can hire a pro to make sure that you did not overlook something. I save thousands by finding things on my own, but when I am going to buy, I look for the pro to insure that there is nothing wrong.

If you find mold indoors, use the tips I have provided in this article to remove the problem. If the mold problem is extremely large and out of hand, have it inspected to make sure that it is not a dangerous strain of mold. Outdoors, remember the pressure washer and it's ability to spray the chemicals to clean the house. If you have a lot of green mold on your siding and deck areas, use a 2 gallon pump up sprayer and from the paint department in most hardware stores, get a product called "Jomax". This added to bleach (follow the label directions) will remove stubborn mold from siding, decks, fences, concrete, stucco, drywall and most surfaces that you would not be afraid to spray with bleach.

Lastly, let me leave you with this…Sometimes water gets into houses in other ways. Busted water pipes, sewage or toilet backups, wet carpets from houses that flood when it rains, broken dishwashers, laundry machines and many other causes that not only let in water but also germs and contamination. For these issues that need treatment for mold, and also for germs, viruses, bacteria and such I have two suggestions. One is called Microban. The other product is called Odoban. To find Microban, you may need to use a search engine to find a local seller of this product. For Odoban, just go to your local Sam's club and find it in the cleaning products section. It costs about $10.00 but will make 30 gallons. Microban runs about $25.00 a gallon. These products both kill mold, mildew, bacteria, viruses and eliminate odors too.

DO IT YOURSELF ADVICE

Most of my seminars are about rehabbing properties for profit as an investor and I usually cover how to hire the work out at a discount rate, therefore you can profit on your own rehabs. I also teach a lot of do it yourself things also. Here are a few topics that you should find helpful to your real estate careers.

When rehabbing property, no matter if it's a plaster wall interior or drywall, consider this. You will probably make the wall repairs using sheetrock. Regular ½ inch sheetrock can run about $8 or $9 per sheet and is great to make rooms new again. I am recommending that for maybe $2 more per sheet, that you get the new sheetrock on the market from Georgia Pacific. It's non-paper surface and also is mold resistant. It has a fiber based facing that actually reduces the chance of mold growth on interior walls. It feels, finishes, sands and performs the same as the sheetrock everyone is used to, but with all the hype out there about mold, I think it's worth the extra dough for the piece of mind it will bring.

Here's a tip that I find very useful in my investing in fixer houses. I try to clean up my houses with a pressure washer and get great results, but sometimes on gutters that are painted white, they have black streaks that just won't come off no matter what. Do you know the streaks I mean? Well I found that if I use a product called Simple Green (about $5) that will remove the stubborn black stains. All I do is spray about a three-foot section, let it sit for a couple of minutes and wipe with a cloth or brush and it disappears. Then I rinse with the garden hose when done.

These products that I mention can be found at most larger hardware stores in your area. And with that, I run across smoke stained walls and ceilings all the time. It's either from nicotine (cigarette smoke) or heaters and chimney smoke. Well hiring this out may cost you a bundle, but do it yourself and save big bucks. Here's what you do. Buy some powdered T.S.P. (tri sodium phosphate) and following the label directions, mix it with warm water and sponge mop the walls and ceilings to clean the sticky problem away. After it dries, you may want to put a coat of primer on the wall and paint with a good latex paint. You can do it!!!

For a nice bead of caulking around bathtub, shower stalls or wherever you need a good looking caulk line, don't fret. Most people I talk to say they can't caulk well at all. Well try this…Use a good brand of caulk (White Lightning or Dap Alex) that is a latex caulk so it cleans up with water and can be painted. To get a pro look from a do it yourselfer you need this tip. Get a small container like a shot glass, put clear dish soap in filling it 2/3 full. Then top off with 1/3 tap water. Now every time you put caulk anywhere, dip your finger in the soap and water solution and then gently drag your finger across the wet caulk and you will get a perfect look every time. The caulk won't stick to your finger either.

Big tip: If you are caulking around your bath tub, fill it with cold water first, then caulk the edges. Then after the caulk dries, let the water out. The weight of the water weighs the tub down and when the caulk is dry and the water is let out, it makes a tighter seal around the tub as it will rise up slightly.

Fixing the edges on wallpaper that's pealing or the edges and seams are loose is a common thing I run across. And sometimes, I paint over wallpaper too. So how would a DIY person stick these little problems down? Easy, Use Elmer's school glue.

That's right, the white stuff you used in school or have bought for your own kids. It works great and the excess glue that may get on the outside of the wallpaper can be sponged away with just water. And if you don't want to stick the edges down and paint over it, you can remove the wallpaper a lot easier by using a scoring tool called a (paper tiger) and then mixing up some Snuggle fabric softener (1 quart) with 2 gallons of warm water and spraying it on the score wallpaper. This will melt the glue underneath and will also amaze your friends too.

Don't like having to paint windows because you get paint all over the glass and then have to spend hours scraping the paint. No more!! Get your car wax from the garage… That's right the Turtle wax or whatever kind of car waxes you have handy. Sponge the wax all over the glass like you would on your car. After the wax dries to a nice chalky white, then paint your windows as fast and sloppy as you want. When the paint dries, just put some newspaper under the window on the floor and using a four in razor scraper, remove the wax and it will fall to the floor as a white dust powder and your windows will easily be clean and look like a pro did the job.

For those ugly rust stains you see in the toilets and bathtubs of fixer properties, most of us want to spend hundreds of dollars getting the surfaces refinished by a pro. But in the spirit of DIY, go get some Lime Away by Lysol. This normally will do the trick and only costs a few dollars per bottle.

This last tip is from my version of do it yourself pest control. Many houses I go in and get totally wiped out by the FLEAS! I just did a bus trip with a group and as we were estimating the repairs, I noticed that my white socks had turned to black from the fleas. Here's a DIY trick…Borax brand laundry soap is very effective on flea problems. Vacuum the carpet well and dispose of the bag. Then sprinkle the Borax laundry detergent all over the carpeted areas. Then work it into the fibers with a broom and leave it for a few days. As I understand it, the borax dehydrates the fleas and therefore kills them, then vacuum the rugs again and throw away the bag. You may need to do this once a week for about three weeks to totally rid the house of fleas, but hey, how many visits does a pest pro have to make at several hundred dollars?

DOES DOOR KNOCKING WORK IN TODAY'S MARKET?

If you are anything like me, then you probably have had many instances of people knocking on your door for one reason or another. I have had people knock to sell Girl Scout Cookies and I don't mind that as I like the cookies and support the cause. However, If you are selling something I am not interested in, then I would rather not be bothered.

Now let's look at door knocking as a whole. My first exposure to door knocking for real estate came from watching my brother Tony Youngs doing it. He is a national expert on Hidden Markets and for over two decades we have been taking people in the field teaching them what we do. We have had great success teaching acquiring and rehabbing properties.

Real estate agents have been using this technique and are taught to use this as a lead generation tactic as well as to get possible listings and get very good results from it. Real estate investors can benefit from this too as this is something not everybody does. Let's go into why door knocking is not exactly a favorite move on people today.

Most investors have a fear of going to doors. They are afraid of what may be on the other side of the door or who may answer. They may be afraid if they hear a dog barking when they knock. Some feel as if the person answering the door will get mad or upset that you are there. This is something that you must get over. As a general contractor going door to door looking for renovation jobs and being with Tony, we have very rarely had a bad experience and we are talking nationwide, not just locally. Statistics show that a face to face conversations get a more positive result by far than just leaving a flyer or such.

That being said, let's get you over the fear of knocking on doors because those who don't do it are losing more than half the deals they could be closing. First you should get with your real estate group and see if they have an expert that teaches a program on knocking. Even better, the expert takes you in the field and takes you to the doors as you watch the instructor do the whole process live in front of you.

Door knocking can be one of the best things in your real estate arsenal if you are taught the do's and don'ts before you try it on your own. There are times of the day that are better than others to knock so you are not too early as people may have a morning routine or need to get kids off to school. If you go too late, they may be in the middle of preparing or eating dinner. Weekdays are always ok but remember more people are home on weekends than during the week due to jobs and such.

You should be taught with a script, but in your conversation you don't want to sound scripted. It makes a difference where you stand as they come to the door so they feel at ease with you. Also, don't go for the kill (hard push) on this visit. You should just open up a conversation and let it go wherever it goes. Go with the flow. Make sure to come off as helpful and friendly and they will open up to you. Remember, if you get with your local real estate group and get an expert that they recommend then door knocking could very well become your best asset in acquiring deals in real estate.

DON'T GET SCAMMED BY CONTRACTORS

As the spring and summer seasons are approaching, many people are looking for contractors to build, remodel or do preventative maintenance on their properties.

Because of this, the opportunity for fraudulent contractors is more frequent as the construction activity is higher. So this is a particularly important time of the year for consumers to take precautionary measures to keep themselves from getting scammed. You may have seen my article in another issue of RIEPS magazine entitled Hiring A Contractor. But for those of you who didn't, here are some tips to protect yourself from contractor fraud.

Year after year, home remodeling fraud costs consumers thousands of dollars and considerable stress and aggravation. Another scary thought is that a big part of the people targeted for this type of scam are elderly persons. Contractor fraud is a criminal activity pulled by scam artists on consumers. They tend to prey on senior citizens and singles, taking advantage of their willingness to trust others who sound believable.

Sadly, it's a different world today. It is best to be cautious when seeking workers.

Among some fairly obvious tactics, here are some things to watch out for.

1. When a person is soliciting door to door for repair work. Though they may seem quite knowledgeable and appear friendly, this is not a common tactic of a pro contractor.

2. They may claim to be working in your neighborhood and just happened to notice some sort of repair needed on your house, such as roofing, painting, or cracked portions in your driveway.

3. A special price or discount may be offered as they claim we are in the area and will knock off a portion of the cost due to excess materials from other contracts.

4. You may also be told you must act right away to get this special discount pricing and you may be asked to give them money up front before starting the work.

More times than not, after receiving a substantial amount of money, these so-called contractors just disappear with the cash. By the time you figure out that they are not showing up, they are long gone, and so is your money. On the other hand, sometimes a contractor will start some of the work and then continuously try to raise the cost of the job causing consumers to be grossly overcharged. See, most people think that since they already signed a contract, they are at the mercy of the contractor. This is why it is so important to screen contractors before you hire them.

Here are some other things that a disreputable contractor may use to scam people:

5. They offer you a discount price if you allow them to use your home to advertise their work. This makes it sound as if they are doing you a favor for a favor.

6. Door to door soliciting leaves very little evidence to track down scammers.

7. Be cautious when someone offers you a lifetime warranty, or long-term promises.

8. Some scammers offer a "free inspection" that always turns up a major repair job.

9. Never fork over a large down payment for materials. 1/3 down is the max.

10. Always insist on a properly written contract, typed, not hand written and signed.

11. Avoid any suspicious contractor whose address is listed as a post office box.

The most important factor is to make sure to thoroughly check out each contractor and to get a contract in writing that spells out even the smallest details. As in several of my other articles, you can't do too much background checking before making a decision. Now don't get me wrong, I am not saying that all contractors are crooked because I am not. I was a reputable contractor for 30 years and most contractors are honest, hard working ladies and gentlemen, however there are thousands all over the country giving good contractors a bad name. Whether you are a senior citizen or a concerned citizen you can get information on how to protect yourself from scams by contacting your local police and there is a great deal of info on the internet.

Some scam artists posing as contractors prey on disasters, such as the recent tornados that devastated many southern states very badly. All of the people who had damaged property are struggling to get their homes repaired and are at great risk of contractor fraud. Workers from all over the country flood areas of disasters hoping for desperate people to let their guard down, knowing that a contractor at your door may be better than waiting weeks to get a contractor to help stop the home from further damage. It is in these situations that most people are scammed. You are vulnerable and desperate, and that's when the scammers are most likely to come in for the kill.

Follow the techniques I stress in my Rehab 101 system to Cowboy Up to scammers.

Always get the contractor's full name, address, business phone and cell phone number. I have been telling people to ask for 5 references from each bidder. The usual 3 that most people ask for, but the fourth is the contractor's material supplier. If the contractor told me he had been in business for 10 years and I call his supplier and he has only been buying from his supplier for 3 months, this indicates a problem. The 5th reference is someone they had to return to fix something for. And if the workers say they have never had to go back to a job, don't believe them. Ask this reference how the workers handled themselves, as they had to come back after the job was finished.

Call the better business office in your local area and inquire about the person or business. You should always get at least three estimates to compare from. Never hire the first person that shows up until you have compared pricing and references. Make sure that they have enough insurance and liability coverage. If you use people without it, make sure to get liability waivers and lien waivers to protect yourself. I never pay more than 1/3 down for a material deposit. This amount should be enough to get the job going. Asking for more is a red flag and should be avoided.

To summarize this article on how to avoid scam contractors, here's a great portion on what things should launch a huge red flag when dealing with contractors.

If the person does not have a listed number in the phone book, and also goes door to door looking for on the spot work requiring money right away. If special prices or discounts are offered but you must act fast. This deal is so we can advertise our work using your home as part of our advertising. If the worker asks you to pull any permits required for the job. And my favorite is, if you pay me in cash I can give you a great discount. Remember the part about having leftover materials from another job and we are passing the savings on to you. More red flags are low-ball offers, sub standard materials, and any funny sounding payment plans. Stick to using contractors whose references check out and remember...IF IT SOUNDS TO GOOD TO BE TRUE, IT PROBABLY IS!!!

ESTIMATING REHAB COSTS IN TODAY'S MARKET

More money is lost in the fix up of properties than any other way, including overpaying when you buy. You can recover from overpaying by saving during the rehab but every dollar spent on the fix up comes straight out of your profit. That's why a big part of my training programs covers the tools as well as the general contractor hires out lower costing labor to do the work and therefore pockets the difference in the cost of what he or she has charged compared to what they pay the lower cost workers. Usually this amount is around 40 to 50% of the bid.

Here is how I direct my clients and members how to get lower costing labor. One way is to hire college students. I put up flyers in the common areas stating what the job is (pressure washing for example) and how much per hour I will pay. I also say that I require 3 references and that he or she must sign a waiver of liability for our protection in case the get hurt. I supply all these forms to my students. Now you are covered as they know what the job is, you check the references and they already have agreed to signing your protection forms as well as how much they will be paid. This in itself saves $300 to $400 by not using high dollar help.

I also love to use older retired people for my jobs instead of general contractors to save literally thousands of dollars over higher cost labor. Here's why I do this. Most retired people did the job you are hiring for maybe 30 years before retiring. Now they are bored and would love to take on some simple jobs just for something to do. Or maybe they would love to earn a little extra cash. I hire them for an average of $20 per hour and I know the job will be done right as the older generation always too pride in what they did and never just did the job half-way. I put up flyers looking for things like this. "Looking for retired plumber to install 2 toilets in rental. I will pay $20 per hour. Call if interested. I use the same for electricians, brick masons, drywallers, painters etc. I put the flyers in bingo parlors, Veterans of foreign wars, moose lodges, elks lodges and so on.

GIVING OLD KITCHENS AND BATHROOM AN INEXPENSIVE FACELIFT

In my long career of being a general contractor and investor, It has been my goal to teach people as many ways as possible to get the highest quality work and results for the lowest possible price. Bringing up the value of an investment property and creating equity are two major factors in building wealth. More profit is lost in the fix up cost of real estate than any other aspect of investing. Therefore making a property look its best without losing your shirt is essential to the rehab business.

One of the most common things I have run across is kitchens and bathrooms with those old stained cabinets. To give the house an inexpensive facelift, I use the following materials and techniques to renew the cabinets to a fresh new and updated look. You may also use these same techniques to do stained trim work, stained doors, windows and paneling. I prefer a white semi-gloss look for updating older homes and the new look can be done for under $100 if you do the following steps from my Rehab 101 system.

First step is to remove all the doorknobs or handles to the cabinets and drawers. Then get a good sponge or cheesecloth and using white vinegar or distilled vinegar full strength, clean all surfaces. This step eliminates oil from cooking over the years and removes any greasy buildup on the surface.

Step two is to get a sanding sponge and use some 200 grit sandpaper to lightly go over all surfaces. You are not trying to remove the stain color, you are just taking the gloss off of all the stained area. Once you are done with this, take a damp cloth or sponge to remove any dust from your project.

The next step is to use an oil based primer such as KILZ or BIN brand and give all surfaces to be painted a good seal coat. This seals in any oils that will secrete through paints in time if not primed right. After your primer dries we will use 100% acrylic latex paint to go over all cabinets and drawers.

I want to stress that I always suggest good quality paint, brushes and materials because you have not saved money or time if you have to do a project twice.

O.K., with my quality brush and roller nap (3/8 inch nap) I will cut in the brushed areas and roll the other areas like normal painting, but here's a great tip…I use Sherwin Williams Pro Classic latex semi-gloss as my finish coat. The reason I choose to use the Pro Classic is that no matter how it is applied, brush-roller or spray, it is a self leveling paint. What that means is that as it dries, it flattens out smooth like an oil base paint and leaves a smooth look with no brush marks.

In my long career of being a general contractor and investor, It has been my goal to teach people as many ways as possible to get the highest quality work and results for the lowest possible price. Bringing up the value of an investment property and creating equity are two major factors in building wealth. More profit is lost in the fix up cost of real estate than any other aspect of investing. Therefore making a property look its best without losing your shirt is essential to the rehab business.

One of the most common things I have run across is kitchens and bathrooms with those old stained cabinets. To give the house an inexpensive facelift, I use the following materials and techniques to renew the cabinets to a fresh new and updated look. You may also use these same techniques to do stained trim work, stained doors, windows and paneling. I prefer a white semi-gloss look for updating older homes and the new look can be done for under $100 if you do the following steps from my Rehab 101 system.

First step is to remove all the doorknobs or handles to the cabinets and drawers. Then get a good sponge or cheesecloth and using white vinegar or distilled vinegar full strength, clean all surfaces. This step eliminates oil from cooking over the years and removes any greasy buildup on the surface.

Step two is to get a sanding sponge and use some 200 grit sandpaper to lightly go over all surfaces. You are not trying to remove the stain color, you are just taking the gloss off of all the stained area. Once you are done with this, take a damp cloth or sponge to remove any dust from your project.

The next step is to use an oil based primer such as KILZ or BIN brand and give all surfaces to be painted a good seal coat. This seals in any oils that will secrete through paints in time if not primed right. After your primer dries we will use 100% acrylic latex paint to go over all cabinets and drawers.

I want to stress that I always suggest good quality paint, brushes and materials because you have not saved money or time if you have to do a project twice.

O.K., with my quality brush and roller nap (3/8 inch nap) I will cut in the brushed areas and roll the other areas like normal painting, but here's a great tip...I use Sherwin Williams Pro Classic latex semi-gloss as my finish coat. The reason I choose to use the Pro Classic is that no matter how it is applied, brush-roller or spray, it is a self leveling paint. What that means is that as it dries, it flattens out smooth like an oil base paint and leaves a smooth look with no brush marks.

My color choice is always white, because clean white cabinets in kitchens and bathrooms make them look brand new and also make the area look larger. Also since it's latex, all my clean up is with simple soap and water. Here's another tip...if your ever having to prime a surface or wall before painting, and your changing the color, have your primer tinted ½ strength of the color your finish coat will be tinted. This eliminates an extra coat of paint trying to cover up white primer. Last, replace all knobs and handles with fresh new hardware for great results, saving hundreds over replacing old cabinets.

HIRING A CONTRACTOR

I am a great believer in "do it yourself" approaches to fixing up properties, but I also feel it is important to hire out what you can't or don't want to do. If you find yourself having to hire a contractor, keep in mind the following guidelines as you make your choice.

You should always get at least three estimates on your project. Statistics show that if you get three estimates, on average there is about a 20% difference between the highest and lowest bid. It also allows you to talk with contractors so you can get a feel for how well you got along with them. When I have met with the contractors, I usually feel better about one of the candidates than the other two, and then I will take the lowest estimate of the three to the contractor I felt best about working with and ask them if they will meet or beat the estimate. Most contractors advertise that they will meet any professional estimate. This is how I manage to get discounts on hiring out work.

Keep in mind that getting free estimates takes up a contractors time, so if you are not ready to start a project yet, wait until you are serious about the job before asking them to show up. If you just want to get an idea of how much something would cost for future reference, call the material suppliers for what you want done and ask what the average going rates are. Example: If you are thinking of getting some siding replaced, look in the yellow pages for companies that sell siding and ask them what the average going rate per linear foot is for siding replacement. This will give you a ball park price.

I always ask for five references from each of the contractors that are giving me a price. Obviously three are for people that they have done work for, but number four should be from their material supplier. I want to ask them about the contractor. I ask them how long the contractor has been a customer. Also if they would recommend the contractor, and has anyone ever complained to them about the contractor. The fifth reference is a customer that needed them to come back to the job to fix something. If they say "we have never had to go back for a problem" that's probably untrue. There are many reasons to have to return to a job, and admitting that they did is a good thing. We want to know from the customer that the contractor stood by his work and came back in a reasonable amount of time and with no attitude about making the job right. In today's market, contractors are too busy or too expensive. My advice will always be to contact the material suppliers of whatever trade you need to hire, and let them recommend a solid contractor who is available at a fair price. Even though I refer to painters here, the same techniques work for all renovation trades, so use this for all types of contractors.

It is important to make sure that you give the same information to each bidder as to what you want to be done. In the business, this is called a "scope of work". This defines exactly what you want to be done, such as "paint all exterior surfaces with two coats of BEHR Paint". All shrubs and hardware to be covered. All glass to be masked from overspray. Shingles to be covered from paint mist. All windows and doors to be painted with two coats semi gloss latex etc. This insures that your estimates are "comparing apples to apples". Everyone bids on the exact same set of details, instead of what each individual contractor wants to do. Always obtain written estimates from each and every bidder. You never want to enter into a verbal contract. It is always best to have agreements in writing and every time you add something to be done, use a form called a "change order". This is agreeing to pay additional money for additional work.

Some areas of the country require that contractors be licensed or registered. You should check what the industry standard is for your area. If your area requires a license, contracts signed by unlicensed or unregistered contractors are unenforceable. Also in these areas, they may require contractors to carry general liability and/or workers compensation insurance. You can call you local insurance agency and ask them what the state requirements are. When you ask for a copy of the insurance letter, don't accept one from the contractor, call the agency that the contractor says insures them and have them send you a letter of insurance. This way you can be assured that the insurance is current and paid up.

Following the format of this article will help you when you need to hire a contractor. Keep in mind the most important things are making sure you have a written contract that spells out the work to be done,

Specify the quality of materials to be used, agree upon the price of the contract as well as how the contract is to be paid and in what kind of money installments, and that if you are requiring license and insurance, all paperwork is in order.

INEXPENSIVE REPAIRS WITH "BONDO"

As I travel around the country giving seminars and training classes on my new SWAT TRAINING VIDEO COURSE, I often get asked if I have a favorite repair technique. The first thing that comes to mind is "BONDO". Yes, the same Bondo body filler that mechanics use to repair dents on wrecked cars. Here's my favorite story:

A man approached me with a problem on his bay window. The window sill had a rotted area about 18 inches long and it also went slightly under the sash. He had gotten estimates to replace his bay window unit for about $2000.00. That included removing the old bay window, supplying and installing the new one and painting it. He asked me if I had any ideas to avoid this costly repair and I told him that I could repair his window for about $10.00 if he would paint the window himself. He was amazed and immediately asked me to proceed. Here's how I did it:

I went to a place that sold auto parts and supplies and bought a quart of "BONDO" Body filler for just under $10. Then I took a screwdriver and dugout all the rotted wood in the area of the window sill. I allowed it to dry (I sped up the process with a blow dryer) and then mixed the Bondo and hardener as per its label directions. Then I scooped the Bondo mixture up and put it in a one-gallon Ziplock baggy. After squeezing the Bondo into the corner of the baggy, I cut the corner of the baggy and used it like a cake decorator would. I slightly overfilled the cavity created from scraping out the rotted wood and then took a paint stir stick (free from anywhere that sells paint) and used it to push the Bondo into all areas needed. After about 10 minutes, the Bondo dried to solid form. Then I used a palm sander with 200 grit sandpaper to sand the widow sill smooth. We took a piece of the window sill that we scraped out that had paint on it to the paint store and had the color computer matched. The man bought a quart of the matched paint and painted the window and it looked as good as new, saving him literally almost $2000.00.

There are hundreds of tips like these in my REHAB 101 system and training and classes. Here are a few more things that you can do with Bondo:

Fill in holes and cracks in plaster walls with Bondo. It's permanent and drywall mud sometimes falls out of plaster wall repairs when disturbed or bumped.

Make repairs in handrails, floorboards, steps, seats and seat backs on decks with Bondo. Then just sand smooth and paint.

For holes in hollow core doors, just fill the hole with tin foil for a backing, spread Bondo generously over the hole and let it dry. Then sand it and paint the door for a permanent fix.

Bondo can also fill cracks in concrete as long as the concrete surface is to be painted afterwards. The color won't match the concrete, therefore you need to paint it. I will sometimes add sand (regular white play sand) to the paint to match the texture of some surfaces.

IT DEPENDS ON THE WEATHER

Almost everything in life is affected by the weather. Real estate is also affected by it. For example, I choose to live in Georgia because I enjoy the warm climate. James prefers to live in Denver because he enjoys the snowy slopes in winter. People in Seattle get rain all the time where in Arizona, not so much.

In places where the weather is severe, the materials used in housing are different from places that don't face the same conditions. This will affect the price of housing and would most certainly raise prices. Let's look at some other ways weather can influence the cost of owning real estate. Living in Georgia where the summer temps can cook an egg on the street, it requires us to use our air conditioners to remain comfortable. I have seen bills adding up to $300 or more in some cases. On the other hand in cold regions, the cost of natural gas and propane are raised very high. Extreme conditions cause us to maintain paint jobs and roofs as well as quality doors and windows to protect our investment.

Weather also impacts our everyday lives in other ways too. We build our schedules around the climate. The restaurants we eat in do their menus based on the weather as it allows certain items only during a short period. Think about how the cost of insurance is based on how much storm damage an area gets. Are you in an area that floods? Are there wildfires common in the area. There are so many things that weather has a real effect on the prices and conditions.

Have you noticed when there is a spike in grocery prices? You can usually pinpoint that to a weather condition somewhere that caused the price increase. Farmers as well as investors in commodities have analysts who perform long range weather forecasts so they can plan how to best take advantage of the good months and prepare for the bad ones.

This has an effect on grains, beans, corn and such. Knowing if there is going to be too much or too little rain will have an impact on our daily costs.

Getting back to real estate, if the weather in an area generally has a lot of rain, I will insist on spending the money for a good gutter system. I need the water to be directed away from the foundation by at least 4 feet to prevent water-damage. I will also want a good quality asphalt shingle roof for protection. If I buy in an area that gets a lot of snow, I would spring for a metal roof and an extremely high quality exterior paint for the house. I would want it to stand up to harsh conditions.

I have been doing a seminar all day here in Tulsa where they have just had a bunch of tornadoes in the area with lots of strong thundershowers. If I was going to buy a property here, I would make sure that it was built with metal studs as opposed to wooden ones. I would spend the extra money to make sure the structure was strong enough to stand up to strong winds. Keep in mind that anytime there is a tornado or an earthquake, the cost of plywood and building materials skyrocket and become scarce in the area. This mean they have to bring it from other areas and supply is low and demand is high. So does weather have an impact on real estate? I think it really does. Not only on the cost to purchase it but also to maintain it.

MAKING HUGE PROFITS WITH MOLD INSPECTION

Those who are familiar with me know that I teach an EPA based mold inspection class as well as that I am certified to teach the lead- based paint RRP renovator course. Not only do I do this in my live trainings at your REIA clubs but it is also in my SWAT home training courses so you can get it without any wait time.

Fast becoming one of my most requested classes, the mold inspection course allows you to be qualified to test properties for molds, toxins, allergens, bacteria, radon and even meth contamination etc. Furthermore, no matter if you choose to do it at home by investing in my SWAT courses or see me live, you receive a certificate of completion after passing a test proving your expertise in mold.

The reason why I started using this as a major strategy in my real estate arsenal is simply this…Every room ever tested shows mold as well as many other elements in the air. The training course gives you the knowledge to test properties (I only suggest vacant bank owned properties) and use this as leverage to get about a 25% discount on the purchase price of your deal.

Without explaining the whole course which takes hours, let me sum it up for you as simply as I can. There are only two ways that a mold test can come back from a lab. One is ELEVATED and the other is NON-ELEVATED. In the live training as well as the SWAT home course you will be taught the types of mold, if they are toxic molds, how to do mold clean up as well as remediation will be explained to you. However so there is no mis-understanding, this course is mold inspection, not remediation. We don't want to do remediation just clean up.

The process works like this. I qualify you to use an air testing machine that collects air samples that are sent into an independent lab for analysis. There is no conflict of interest or liability on your part because all you do is collect the sample. And you are qualified to do that. The independent lab then sends you a report sometimes listing up to 10 or 15 types of molds, toxins allergens etc. It will also mention that these molds have been known to cause illness in some cases and they recommend (not require) remediation.

Here is the step by step, but keep in mind, you can't do this without the course being completed as then you have no qualification and it becomes just your opinion.

First you take my mold inspection course either live or from my SWAT courses. Then find a vacant bank owned house and make a reasonable offer to get your foot in the door. In your offer ask for a 10 day inspection period for rehab estimates and such. During this time is when you so your air sample collection and send to the lab. This costs about $40 to test and you overnight the sample and ask the lab return the results by e-mail. Once the property has been declared elevated, you seek a mold remediation estimate to remediate the kitchen. The kitchen is where I always test because it gives the highest estimate.

Now I re-submit my offer to the bank MINUS the amount of the mold remediation estimate. I supply the bank with the estimate as well as the mold test to back up my lower offer. Now get this cause this is the secret…The bank now has to sell you the property for your price or huge discount OR they by law must disclose a copy of the mold estimate and the lab test to all who have made offers and all new offers coming in. The banks do not want to advertise they have a mold problem that may cause illness to someone.

So they choose most often to sell to you. Then instead of remediation, my class teaches you mold CLEAN-UP so you can clean the kitchen area and re-test. Send in the test after the mold clean up it then comes back non-elevated. So you got your huge discount and a non-elevated test that you now can disclose saying you tested for mold and here are the non elevated results.

Well there it is in as simple as I can explain, but please do not try this without coming to the class first! You can increase your profit by an average of 20K using this technique. You can also use your certificate to get a license to do this as a business for another income stream charging $250 to $350 per test. Remember you can also do this at home with my major SWAT rehab course.

OUTLINE FOR A BASIC HOME RENOVATION

- Improve curb appeal by removing junk and debris in yard.

- Mow lawn, trim bushes, edge curb and driveway

- Pressure wash exterior, decks, fence and driveway.

- Make sure that power is on and available for workers.

- If bathrooms are not useable, supply a portable one.

- Secure a dumpster in a reasonable area if one is needed.

- Trash out interior, exterior, garage, basement and attic.

- Pull any and all permits needed for all aspects of work.

- Do all demolition interior and exterior at this point.

- Now do any structural work or framing if required.

- Talk to inspector about details and schedule inspection.

- This could take a few days to 2 weeks weather permitting.

- If needed, install windows and exterior doors at this point.

- Give one to two days for this portion to be completed.

- If mechanicals are needed do HV/AC, plumbing, electrical.

- Do those in that order and allow 2 to 3 days to complete.

- Install any insulation that may be needed throughout.

- Allow one day for this and make sure no corners are cut.

- Make sure that all inspections have been done by now.

- Drywall installation is the next step. Hang and finish mud.

- In cooler weather, warm area for drying. Allow 2 days.

- This is the best time to apply primer to the drywall.

- Now paint before any cabinets or trim are installed.

- If new cabinets are needed allow 1 to 3 days for this.

- Have all countertops installed in bath, kitchen etc.

- Make sure all inspections to this point are done.

- Paint all doors, trim and any other areas to finish.

- At this point install any shelving or hardware needed.

- Now painting is complete, install your flooring choices.

- The next step is to touch up paint anywhere needed.

- Have a final cleaning of all areas of the house.

- If doing a new roof, do so before exterior painting.

- If needed, now is the time to paint exterior of house.

- Stain or seal any decks or fences to protect the wood.

- Address any issues with driveways or walkways last.

- Make sure that you have met codes and inspections.

PAINTING OVER WALLPAPER

I cut corners every chance I get to save money on my rehab investments. One of the things that I do is to paint over wallpaper when possible. As long as you follow my steps below, you should have no problem getting a pro finish that will last for years to come.

STEP 1: Make sure all the edges and seams are glued down tight. I have found that most pro's in the business carry Elmer's school glue to stick down and loose paper (or vinyl in most cases) and repair seams. This is the white glue that is non toxic and water clean up.

STEP 2: Use blue tape, referred to as long mask and may be left on a surface up to a week without removal problems. Tape off all mirror frames, doorknobs, window and door trim as well as baseboards etc.

STEP 3: If your wallpaper has a bright pattern, you may want to prime the surface with an oil based primer to kill the colors from bleeding through the paint. If you are painting a tinted color, you can have the paint dept. tint your primer to the color of your paint. This will eliminate painting multiple coats.

STEP 4: This step is very important to make sure that you do not have a difference in color shade between the cut in portion and the roller portion. The biggest rule of painting with the best results is to always roll into a wet edge. Most of us will cut in the room with a brush and then roll the room. This is wrong...Cut in one wall, then roll that wall. Allowing the cut in to dry before you roll will give a color shade difference when you roll into it, basically being two coats where you overlapped with your roller. Doing one wall at a time will give you the wet edge you need for the brush and roll to dry at the same pace.

STEP 5: Use a three speed fan, set on medium to blow at the wall as you paint each wall. Most wallpaper has a tendency to bubble up as the paint dries. Using the fan slows down the drying of the paint and it will stop the bubble effect on the wall. Even if it bubbles just a little at first, the fan will make the bubbles disappear when fully dry.

STEP 6: Use a latex paint that is acrylic and water based whether you used a primer first or not. This way anytime you need to repaint, you can just use latex right over the previous paint. Also, your clean up will be easier and your paint tools will clean up with just soap and water.

STEP 7: Allow the paint to dry totally before putting on a second coat (if needed) or before removing the tape from the protected areas. When you remove the tape, sometimes it is important to use a razor knife to cut along the line where the tape and paint meet. This way you will not pull any paint up as you remove the tape.

STEP 8: This is my final step before cleaning up the area and moving on. I had removed the light switch cover plate before painting. Before I put it back, I will place a small piece of masking tape on the back. On this tape, I will smear a color sample of the paint I used for that room on it. I will also write the color code used for tinting and the store I got the paint from. Therefore, even if the paint can gets lost…I will always have the color code to have the same paint made for next time, or a sample that the store can computer match for me. This works great if you are as forgetful as I am sometimes.

THE POWER OF TWO

Being in the real estate and seminar business for over two decades has taught me a lot over the years. I have shared the stage with numerous famous people in the biz, and have learned that there is much that goes on behind what you actually see. Many of my friends who do training classes and boot camps are married and also have other businesses besides the public training. Like myself and wife Barb, you have to keep it all running smoothly. You must become a "power couple" to make an impact on your life and others.

It had always been a dream of mine to travel around teaching others about real estate. As you know, I travel all over the country teaching rehab to thousands of people, so I got my wish. But I must tell you, your spouse really has to be on board with you and share in helping to impact other people's lives for the better. Let me share with you a little of the behind the scenes of "the power of two".

As a couple for seventeen years now, my wife Barb and I have tried to be a positive force together. As individuals, we could be rather mundane. But as a couple we are much more. We have donated my Rehab 101 courses to many Habitat For Humanity chapters nationwide as well as worked on the properties. Barb also has helped many cancer patients to find optional treatments that they were not aware of, not even from their own doctors. We try to help as many people as we can reach, no matter if it is for big or small reasons.

We live in Georgia and recently a law was coming into effect that most of the general public did not know about. It was a law that would make it illegal for investors in Ga. To hire people to fix up properties without having a contractors license. This would also require classes and testing to pass the license exam. It would make my 80 year old neighbor lady a criminal for hiring a plumber to fix her toilet as she had all her life and she would not even know she was breaking the law.

As we are members of our local investment club, we were contacted by some members and told of this law that very few knew about to see if we could make some sense out of it. After all, I was Mr. Rehab and Barb can move mountains if she needs too. So immediately we had an e mail blast to all the investors as well as placing ads and getting the word out there that Barb and I were going to book a hotel ballroom and have any and all investors in Ga. Come out to see what this really meant to all of the citizens who live here. Barb contacted the Secretary of state as well as license board officials and so called experts on the interpretation of the laws and how it would impact us. I would host the panel and ask questions as well as direct questions from the public to the panel.

Barb and I paid all the costs for the ballroom, officials and such because it affected us as well as our community. The crowd got really upset with the way the govt. interpreted the new rules. According to them, investors and homeowners could not hire anyone to do work on homes without having a general contractors license. To do so you could be fined and also charged with a crime. This would put us all out of business. Or even homeowners would need a license to hire any work out.

Armed with notes and questions, an angry Barb spent the next several days contacting senators, congressmen, and city officials or anyone who had their name attached to this bill. After many phone calls and e-mails Barb ripped people apart over the pure stupidity of what we were told.

She would not let this go. Finally the person who wrote the bill had a conversation with her and explained that the intent of this was not intended to apply to investors and homeowners. It was supposed to control people who actually did contracting for a living. Investors and homeowners do not charge people for contract work as a service or a business. So we had exemptions to the rules. This was great news and we had all the e mails and such from the people who wrote the bill to show the original panel that they had misinterpreted the intent of the new rules and relayed incorrect info to us.

Barb and I immediately spread the new that we were putting together more ballroom meetings that would be free to the public so we could inform them of the correct news. We took a stand for our community and ourselves and got results. So maybe not to all, but to some, we for a few moments were a power couple.

Switching gears a little here, here is more of the power of two. When you see me speaking across the country at seminars and other real estate events, I need you to know how I got there. We share all our businesses as equals. My part is to get out there and teach people how to rehab property. Barb had to book my airline, hotel and rental car and I have done up to 200 events per year. For this reason and to help our business she became a licensed travel agent. Now she brings in a lot of extra income for doing what she did anyway before.

Barb and I look at the properties we invest in together and if we buy it, my part is to get it fixed up to rent or sell. Her part is to show the house if we are selling, or to check out the people we rent to. Sometimes when I am speaking, she will run the sales in the back of the room and process them.

So you may know a lot more about me from my bio, seminars or even if you have "googled" me. What you don't know is that Barb also handles our shipping and receiving of products. She is in charge of production as well as all our accounting coming in or out. She does our taxes for all our businesses as well as being my booking agent for all my events. Our events that we do with a partner called "investor bonanza" she and Noreen act as seminar coordinators as Don and I are the promoters.

It is a whole lot easier to run the business when I am in town, but when I am on the road; Barb runs the office and staff. I just want you to know that I have not even touched the tip of the iceberg on the amount that Barb makes our business side work so well. Barb and I have built a lifestyle that we both love. We travel to places I never dreamed we would go. We are very successful together and have bonded with other power couples in this business that know, it takes the power of two to get to this level of enjoyment in life. Barb is my wife, my life and my best friend. I could not be me, without her. The power of two.

PROSPECTUS FOR PRIVATE MONEY LOANS

1. You MUST have the property under contract before applying! Otherwise there is no deal for prospective lenders to consider.

2. The terms of the contract must be clearly stated in the offer. This includes purchase price and a specific closing date. Ex. 30 Days

3. The after repair value (ARV) must be documented to show profit This includes comparable sales and days on market till sold.

4. If using a real estate agent, include listing document for details. Lender will need to know who pays commission affecting profit.

5. All lenders require that renovation estimates be submitted. Profit potential can not be determined without fix up costs.

6. Our lenders limit is 65% to 70% of the after repair value of house and is secured by placing a lien on subject property as collateral.

7. The interest rate they receive is 10% interest only paid monthly. Unless specified otherwise, principal to be repaid in 12 months.

8. The money used to purchase the property is sent to the seller. This is done to insure the money gets to the seller securing deal.

The basic guidelines above will give borrowers an idea of what they need before expecting to be considered for private money.

A common misconception is they hear " we loan money for deals" and immediately think it's any deal. You can't just contact a realtor and say Hey send me some deals, I have a money lender. First, we will but rarely fund properties listed with realtors. We buy wholesale deals not RETAIL. We focus on "fix and flip" deals so we get our money back quick and re loan it.

Always remember THE DEAL IS BASED ON THE INFO YOU PROVIDED before asking for a loan. The more you provide the better your chances.

Borrower. You may have the best intentions but lenders only look at the numbers and profit and your job as borrower.

PUT THOUSANDS OF DOLLARS OF PROFIT IN YOUR POCKET WITHOUT DOING THE WORK YOURSELF!

Regardless of which real estate investment strategy you use to create your wealth, you have to control whose pocket the money is flowing into. So you ask." How can I put thousands of dollars MORE in my pocket WITHOUT doing the work myself? Well, I am a successful contractor and investor who can show you how to create HUGE PROFITS in properties you thought had little or no profit, and create MASSIVE EQUITY in all your properties.

Part of my expertise is teaching people how to rehabilitate properties for 50 to 75% off of the normal estimated cost. My knowledge and ability to get the highest quality results for the absolute lowest possible price has earned my company many prestigious renovation contracts such as Courtyard By Marriott hotels, The 1996 Atlanta Summer Games, Two contracts with communications giant MCI, Publix Distribution Center, Fidelity National Banks, Blimpie Restaurants and hundreds of single and multi-family homes nationwide.

I know that buying any type of discount property insures a lower purchase price and I can teach you valuable contractor tips and techniques to LOWER your FIX UP and MAINTENANCE costs by 50 or even 75%! You will literally add THOUSANDS to your net worth and your equity position whether you own one home or one hundred homes.

I teach 101 valuable techniques, which range from minor cosmetics for the new investor, to MAJOR REHABS for the seasoned investor. My REHAB 101 system is designed to save both time and money on all types of rehab and maintenance projects. So whether you like DO IT YOURSELF techniques, or want to HIRE THE WORK OUT for a fraction of the going rate, Rehab 101 is a must for your investment career arsenal.

Specializing in teaching others how to ACT AS THEIR OWN GENERAL CONTRACTOR, I stress that getting contractor discounts, hiring out what you can't do and using do it yourself tips can dramatically increase the profit to be made on distressed properties nationwide.

Did you know that a general contractor makes his profit by sub-contracting the repair work to be done, he oversees the job. Handles the material buying and pockets up to 50% or more of the jobs estimated cost. Most general contractors do none of the work themselves. Learn how to put those profits in YOUR POCKET without having to do the work yourself!

MORE PROFIT IS LOST IN THE FIX UP OF PROPERTIES THAN ANY OTHER AREA! I TAKE GREAT PRIDE IN HELPING OTHERS BECOME MORE SUCCESSFUL IN THEIR INVESTMENT CAREERS BY TEACHING HOW TO SAVE TIME, MONEY & INCREASE THE VALUE AND EQUITY OF PROPERTY.

QUICK, INEXPENSIVE ROOF REPAIRS

When you have a damaged roof, time is of the essence. The first thing is to make sure that the roof does not leak as this will cause more damage to the home and it's contents. If you have a leak, move anything of value out of the area and catch the water with whatever you can until you can stop the leak.

I recommend that you always have a blue tarp that is large enough to cover a major portion of your roof just for such emergencies. They are inexpensive and it could be days, even weeks before the roof can be properly repaired.

Here are some suggestions for fast, do it yourself roof repairs that are easy and inexpensive to do. If you have asphalt shingles that have blown off and don't have any spares, then check with your larger hardware chain for matching the shingles. I always recommend that you keep at least one bundle of shingles for repairs. If you need to replace any plywood, never replace with piecework. Always use a full sheet (4'x8') exterior grade and in most cases, it should be 5/16 or better. Before you put down the shingles, make sure that your # 15 felt is in good condition. I do not recommend using staples on shingles. I prefer to use 12 gauge hot dipped galvanized roofing nails measuring 1 ¼" in length.

For smaller leaks and repairs around roof vents, skylights and seams I like to use roof cement or black vinyl that comes in tubes as well as gallons and five gallon sizes. This product can be used in wet or dry conditions. You can literally put it on totally wet surfaces. It can be used with a caulk gun in tube form, or troweled on in the canned forms. Any place that you make a repair that it joins the house siding or chimney and such, you may need to install aluminum flashing under your repair area to waterproof gaps between roof material, siding and other roof venting protuberances.

If you have flat roofs or mobile homes that have leaks, you can use Kool Seal

Roof Patch®, for large deep areas. After that you can use regular Kool Seal Elastomeric® coating to waterproof your entire flat roof. If your flat roof is covered in tar and gravel, then use roof tar for your repairs. Remember that thicker is better, so make sure that you don't get some real thin tar based liquid, as it will ooze through the cracks and repairs requiring more than one application. On metal roofs you may also use thick tar based products. And for membrane roofs or Ethylene Propylene Diene Monomer (EPDM roofs) use products called Liquid Roof® or Liquid Rubber EDPM® to make your repairs. Note that these coatings can be rolled on or use an airless spray gun.

As a general contractor turned investor it has been my goal to teach people as many ways as possible to get the highest quality work and results for the lowest possible price. To bring up the value of an investment property, create equity and protect that investment are the three major factors in building wealth.

REAL ESTATE CRUISES,
MY FAVORITE NETWORKING

Most any serious real estate investor will agree that one of your most valuable tools in being successful is the art of networking. In many cases the first thing I would advise is to join your local real estate investment club. This gives you access to many like minded people who like you want to buy, sell trade and rent properties.

I look forward to the National REIA cruise and have been aboard for this networking cruise for almost two decades now. As a faithful follower of National, I have become friends and established great relationships with the staff as well as the hundreds of attendees who flock to this unique event. If you have not attended before, you are missing out on loads of opportunities presented here.

Let me give you some benefits of a real estate related cruise that you may not have considered. The cruise is education based and packed full of real estate strategies for you to learn in a relaxed atmosphere. The event if you care to keep receipts and records of meetings and such is something that may be able to be written off as business and education. There are many opportunities for you to network with others during lunches, dinners, breaks and the many social functions that are planned throughout the cruise.

Since you have all this information and personal contacts, you can easily prepare your years business plan based on what you learn here. I am a national speaker so I use this time to network with REIA clubs to have me as a guest speaker at events all over the country. I also make many priceless contacts to strengthen my wealth team. I find people to buy from, sell to, speak for as well as making lifetime friends at these events. This will lead to multiple business and friendly relationships, some of them will change your life.

My attending the real estate cruises has brought me some of the best friends I have in my life. Though I can't list them all, or all their credentials, here are just a few of the life changing and lifelong relationships my wife Barb and I have built from people we met on cruises.

Carl and Vicki Fischer have become a big part of our investment team as well as travel partners. Carl is Principle of CAMAPLAN, a company that handles self-directed IRA's and 401 K as well as many more investment opportunities. They are partners of Barb and I in multiple ways and handle a portion of our portfolio. As friends, we also travel the world together exploring places we only dreamed of.

Mike and Beth Butler are also friends and partners of ours that we met while cruising more than 15 years ago. Mike is an expert on Land-lording as well as quick-books for real estate and has authored many courses and training materials on these topics and more. He also wrote best selling books on real estate related topics. Mike and Beth mentor me on aspects of my career in web design as well as marketing, planning and so much more. Mike and Beth also arrange mastermind sessions with Carl, Vicki, Barb, myself and the next couple I will mention at least once or twice a year so that we can all offer our clients the best and newest information available as we are all national trainers and Mentors.

The next I will mention (as there are so many over the years) would be another long -time relationship. Larry and Pam Goins. Larry is well known for his training courses such as "The Ultimate Buying Machine" and "Filthy Riches" just to name a few. Larry and Pam are also travel all over with all of us. We all enjoy sharing ideas and helping each others businesses grow so we can be the best at what we do. And how could I not bring up our other friends from the Goins Group, Matt and Kandas Broome. Both are great friends and have brought much insight to all we do. Kandas is almost magical at keeping us on top of our game and Matt is our sounding board. What a team!

As for myself, I am known as Mr. Rehab, a general contractor of 30 years turned investor about 25 years ago. I teach rehabbing properties for about 50% off regular contractor rates and give Home Depot tours, estimating property tours, bootcamps and speak for Reia clubs nationwide. My latest and best training course is called SWAT. Secret Ways And Techniques. But enough about me. My brother Tony Youngs brought me into real estate investing. Tony is a Master of Hidden Market properties and unlisted properties no one else can find. He also is one of the top rated one on one trainers in the country and his success rate from students is

Now that brings me to this portion of why you should choose to network all the time, anywhere and everywhere. Carl, Vicki, Barb and I are on a 21 day cruise from Seattle to Australia. And guess what??? It's a write off!!!

First off, we are both clients of each other. This means that we are taking this as a business related trip and our purpose is real estate as well as investing. At all our dinners and lunches we are making contacts with people who have offered us places to stay for rent in Hawaii, Fiji and Australia as we are stopping at all of the areas. I am picking up the tab on a lot of my clients costs as well as him mine.

We are making contacts to broaden our portfolio's buy seeking properties at all our stops. We are looking for vacation homes as well as rentals, commercial buildings business opportunities and such. Sure we are having a blast on the cruise and the foods great and the contacts are endless.

In a nutshell, it works like this. No matter what you are doing, make it about real estate or business. Our goal is to find properties in these very desirable areas so that we may use them as AirBnB. We are looking for anything to build our business deals and our property ownership. Cruises are my favorite way to vacation. Now it is my favorite way to network. And If you can write it off as business with people you enjoy hanging out and working with, it's all good!!!

RELATIONSHIPS THAT BUILD WEALTH

Anyone who has been in the real estate business for any time will tell you that the more people you have that can help you, the better. Investing in single family or multi-unit housing is not an individual task, however you can do it by yourself. You just have to surround yourself with good business relationships. The more quality, professional people you can gather to help you will ensure that your success rate will skyrocket.

One of the most important aspects of being in real estate is that you must have a plan, or for most people, a system. My plan has always been that I am a rehabber. I buy homes, condo's or multi-unit structures to remodel and then rent or sell them. Because of my general contractor background, I was able to excel not only in the investment side, but also the teaching side of real estate. My strategy these days is that my focus is buying REO properties. Here are the relationships that fuel my business to a great level of success.

One of the most important people in your business should be a mentor. This can be anyone you want. They don't have to be a pro or someone that charges you a fee for advice. This could be as simple as your father, a brother, sister, uncle or whatever. As long as you respect the thoughts and actions as well as the opinions of this person and are willing to perform in the same manner as this person, then they can help you make your way through your career.

Another important relationship would be a personal coach. A coach is someone that holds you accountable for your actions. They can give you advice as well as instruction. They can motivate you or back you down if needed. When I am coaching someone, we come up with short term goals, long term goals and strive to meet these a little bit at a time. A coach is someone that you have to report your progress to, and prove to them that you are capable of reaching the goals you have set for yourself and your future.

My favorite person that I have on my wealth team is my broker. She is just the best. This broker has contacts with several banks and for these banks she is the BPO. For those who do not know a BPO is a broker's price opinion. This is the amount of money that the broker recommends that the bank sell the house for in the current market. Also as a broker, the banks will provide a list of properties in their inventory that they are going to sell in a certain time frame and she is to list and show these properties until they sell. What you want to do is create a relationship with one of these type brokers and get on their "buyers list." This is a list of investors that the broker reveals the property addresses and selling info in order for us to make offers on these deals. Make sure that your broker is also an investor for best results.

The next person you need to have is a real estate agent. This person is a different asset to you than the broker. The agent is more for valuable info on the properties and the broker is more for getting you the properties to buy. You agent can make offers for you or list your homes to get you buyers. Your agent can run a "comparable market analysis" (cma) on your property that tells you how much a like property would sell for. It will also tell you about how many days it would take to sell, and they may have some insight on what areas you would want to buy and sell in.

All of us need to have a great attorney. Mine is, and yours should be a real estate lawyer and hopefully an investor too. This way they would be well versed on if you are allowed to do double closings, subject to deals and the foreclosure laws as well as other things that would be pertinent to your city and state. They can assist you in closings as well as prepare your warranty deeds. Quit claim deeds, deeds of trusts, deed in lieu of foreclosure as well as other related terms. A good attorney is worth his or her weight in gold, and sometimes the fees seem as if they are.

I have created many relationships with bird dogs. A bird dog is someone who finds deals for you to buy. Normally they do this for a finder's fee or a piece of the profit. My bird dogs are more often than not, trained by me personally. However most of them have obtained some sort of formal training prior to becoming a bird dog. In many conversations I have had with investors over the years the average fee paid to a bird dog is about $500 for finding a suitable deal. I am not talking mansions here, I am talking bread and butter easy deals with a modest amount of profit. Obviously the more expensive the home and higher profit, the more money you pay for your fee. So if you have cash but no time to hunt for deals, then a bird dog is a nice alternative to not getting deals at all.

I have a wonderful accountant. She happens to be my wife, Barb. Having a great accountant really helps in this business. She keeps me up to speed on what needs to be paid and when. She knows how much is coming in and when. I have available to me the budgets we have to invest with and I know in advance what kind of deals we can buy or fund. She works directly with my tax pro at tax time. Together they work out my land trusts and LLCs. It's like having a cpa staff at your beckon call for all your money matters, tax wise or other.

If you can, try and make your relationship with your banker like I have. I can call my banker on the phone and have things done that most people spend hours waiting to be done. One reason is simply this. One of my banks is a credit union. They usually are easier to work with than normal banks and the rates are normally lower too. I have found that loans (in my experience) are much easier to get. Here is what I love about my banker. If I need 10K in certified funds to buy a property, I can call on the phone and tell her what I need and by time I get to the bank, she has the check ready and waiting for me. Another thing that I love about being in tight with my banker is that I can call in a loan. If I want a loan I can call her and tell her the amount I need and what I need it for. She gets the ball rolling and has me pre-approved so that when I get to the bank, my loan has already been processed and I sign a few documents and within minutes have my check. Keep in mind that I have been banking here for years, so make good friends with the top person at your bank and make sure to talk face to face with that person as if they were your best friend every time you go in. sooner than you think, you will be known by the employees of that bank. Also if I deposit a large check, most banks put a 10 day hold on it. My banker waves this hold because they see me in the bank all the time. This could work for you too.

My wife has a great relationship with our financial advisors. Yes we have more than one. One of them came from my side of the family, as my dad had been using this person for years. I followed my dad's advice to use this guy for our personal stock and bond investments. The other person is out of state and comes from my wife's side. He has expertise in real estate holding, stocks, bonds, muni's as well as many other investments that I was not familiar with. Through his type of investing, Barb and I have obtained substantial wealth that without the ideas of this man we never would have gotten involved. I had no interest or knowledge in the investments he has made on our behalf. Now I am a big fan and really hope that all of you will take advantage of a financial advisor.

I could go on and on about who is important and who is not, but I will summarize by saying this. Obviously I want you to have good contractors. Call material suppliers such as paint stores and drywall supply houses for recommendations of contractors. A good landscaper can change a houses appearance for very little money. A hard money lender who has reasonable rates is a must for real estate investors. Make sure to include an appraiser and a mortgage company in your strategy. And last, make sure and join your local investment club. Once you join, you have access to all of the people above and more. You have people who want to buy property and people who want to sell. You have access to partners, lenders, agents and many other real estate related opportunities. Normally the cost is very inexpensive, but the potential of being in a room full of like-minded people and using the assets available to you is beyond helpful it's downright successful.

THE REMODELING CONTRACT

Only a written contract protects both the Homeowner and the Contractor. Therefore, your Contractor should put in all agreements and any oral arrangements made during the negotiations in writing on the contract. This is the most important item that will hold the project together and makes sure all parties are in agreement of the scope and final vision of the project. If it is not in the contract it does not in the eyes of the court exist. Make sure all parties initial all pages of the final and set contract.

Here is a list of specific things to look for in the contract before signing:

- The Contract should include the contractor's name, address, telephone and license number.

- The contract should have a time frame. Include approximate start and a substantial completion date.

- Never under any circumstances sign a blank or partially blank contract. Both you and the contractor are bound by what is in writing on the contract. Do not leave blanks to be filled out later or with the phase TBD. Read it carefully and thoroughly before signing. If you have questions or unclear of wording, have it explained to your satisfaction before signing. Make sure all of the financial terms have been agreed upon and that they are clearly written. Once you have signed – MAKE A COPY FOR YOURSELF and keep it for your records.

- Make sure all financial terms are spelled out in the contract and both you and the contractor are clear on them. The total price, payment schedule and any cancellation penalty should be clear. Have an understanding how the Contractor will invoice you. Note: You should expect to pay 1/3 of the total contract as a down payment. Payments after should be determined prior to the signing of the contract. Either weekly, monthly or at set completion stages.

- Contract should specify all materials to be used, quality, color, weight, size, brand name and quality.

- Never under any circumstances sign a blank or partially blank contract. Both you and the contractor are bound by what is in writing on the contract. Do not leave blanks to be filled out later. For example, the contract should say "install oak kitchen cabinets manufactured by AAA, Inc. according to plan, "not just "install kitchen cabinets".

- If a warranty is offered, get it in writing and read it carefully. A warranty must state whether it is limited (meaning repairs, replacements, or refunds are limited in some way), or full (one that will repair or replace the product or refund your money within a certain time period). The warranty should spell out all terms and conditions in a way that you can understand them. It should specifically say by name whom will honor the warranty – the contractor, the dealer or the manufacturer. The warranty must include the name and address of the party offering it and the duration of coverage. Warranties for products such as appliances or cabinets are passed through the manufactures.

- Your Contract should include everything you think is important. Some items that may seem miniscule now may become a hurdle later. The list below may have some items that you might want to think of including:

- Complete clean up and removal of debris and materials

- Any special request such as saving lumber (for firewood) and unneeded material or old appliances and fixtures (to reuse).

- Any special instructions regarding pets, children, areas where materials may be stored, or landscaping to be temporarily moved.

- Security – who gets keys or access codes and what means of security will be taken when a wall might be knocked down.

Federal law requires a contractor to give homeowners written notice of their rights to, without penalty, cancel a contract within three business days of signing it, provided was solicited at some place other than the contractor's place of business or appropriate trade premises – the homeowners residence, for instance. This is your Right of Rescission.

The contract should include procedures for handling change orders during the course of the project.

A binding arbitration clause is also a good inclusion in the event a disagreement occurs. Arbitration enables both parties to resolve disputes more quickly and effectively without costly litigation.

Request a contractor's Affidavit of Final Release be provided to you at the time you make the final payment, or obtain final lien waivers from all subcontractors and suppliers. These are your assurances that you will not be liable for any third-party claims for nonpayment of materials or subcontractors.

The items below are RED Flags that a Contractor might not be someone you want to deal with:

- You cannot verify the name, address and telephone number or credentials of a contract.

- The salesperson tries "high-pressure" to have you sign a contract by using scare tactics, intimidation or threats. (Remember you have 3 days to cancel a contract). The salesperson tells you this is a special price available today only if you sign.

- The contractor does not comply with your request for references, or the references have some reservations about a job the contractor did.

- You are unable to verify that the contractor is licensed or insured and the law requires such.

- Beware of anyone who tells you that the Federal Housing Administration or any other government agency approves or endorses a remodeler's work

- You are asked to pay for the entire job in advance or to pay cash to a salesperson instead of using a check, credit card or money order to the company itself

- You are asked to sign a completion certificate for the job before it is properly and fully completed.

Remember to protect yourself at all times. Getting multiple estimates is always a good idea to get a good selection and a better price. And as always (get it in writing).

THE SCOPE OF WORK
(Don't get an estimate without one!)

When buying distressed properties, one of the most important things you will need before getting repair estimates is a "scope of work". A scope of work is a detailed list of repairs to be done and the fashion in how they are done. The main benefits to having a good scope are that you give the same scope to each bidder. Therefore, the bids can be compared as "apples to apples". Everyone bids on the exact same thing so then you can concentrate on the best contractor at the lowest price.

In my Rehab 101 training, I use my property inspection forms to compile a detailed scope of work. There are several things needed to build the best scope and I will give you some good guidelines to go by for yours. You must first list all the materials needed for each aspect of the job. If you are doing painting, list what brand of paint to be used, oil or latex, one or two coats, sprayed or brushed and rolled and so on. The more details the better. However, you should be able to describe your scope of work in just a few paragraphs.

As in all contracts, the scope should describe who is supposed to perform each article of work. That way there is no confusion as to what is expected of each person hired on the job. For example, if you are roofing the house and also having some carpentry repairs done and you find that some plywood needs replacing before the new shingles are put down, you must assign who is to replace the plywood…the roofer or the carpenter.

Aside from the choosing of who is to be given each job, you must also be very detailed about what they are to do and not to do. You might have someone putting in a new ceiling fan and changing a few light fixtures and such, and this is fine. But you need to draw the line and list that this person is not to do any electrical that requires wiring into the main service panel. The difference being that in most states anyone can do fans, light and switches, but to wire into the panel box requires a licensed person and possibly a permit. Set the limits on what they are allowed and not allowed to do.

We have talked about the who and the what portions of a scope of work. Now let's talk about "when". This is the part of a scope that tells when the job will start. It tells when the job will be finished. You can set the daily working hours to suit you and also can detail if Saturday and or Sunday are considered working days. Some people Do not want to have workers on their jobs on Sundays as that is a personal day to many. In most cases, I will let the worker give me the timeline that they think the job will take. Let's say I was told the job would take two weeks to complete. I will agree to this but in my contract I may have a clause that says "contractor is to complete this job satisfactorily in two weeks. After a one-week grace period beyond these two weeks a $50.00 a day penalty will be deducted from the balance due until job is completed. Just to make sure that the job does not linger too long or in case you have a contractor who abandons the job, this will eliminate your liability for liens or owing money to the contractor.

Another aspect of the scope of work should lay out the payment schedule. There are many common ways to have this set up. One of the most common payment plans is one third of the contracted amount down, with the remaining balance due on completion. This allows most contractors the ability to buy the materials needed for the job without coming out of their own pockets. Some people are wary of giving some money up front as in some stories we have all heard about someone running off with the money and never starting the job. But think of it this way. If you have done your homework before hiring someone, you'll know if they are to be trusted. The reason I will give the one third up front is because if I have given them the money to buy the materials, then I have less worry that anyone can put a lien on the property for the materials used. If they paid for them up front…no lien. You may also choose to pay on draws or the amount of work completed. You can pay on Fridays, or you can pay at the 25% complete, 50% complete and final payment.

Remember to get you lien releases signed every time you issue a check.

When listing the materials to be used and the method of application you must be very specific to avoid misunderstanding. If you are having siding installed you want to list exactly what type you agreed to. Is it Hardi-plank or regular Masonite? Is it textured, beveled or T-111? Make sure the details are there. If doing a new roof then you want to know the same type of things… "the shingles to be used are Sovereign brand, 25 year shingles at $35.00 per square from Home Depot". Something like that for each item to be done to the house. Now you also want the application of items to be described. For the siding, are they using hammers or nail guns? You want to know this because nail guns can be set to different settings that regulate how the nail ends up in the siding. If set too strong, the nail heads go too far into the siding and this will allow water to get into the siding at every nail and will start to cause your siding to rot out almost immediately. Or for the roof…is it a roof over (putting shingles on top of the existing ones) or is it a tear off (scraping all old shingles and felt down to the plywood and starting new).

The last part of a good scope of work is the final acceptance of the work and materials done on a property. You want to make sure that all code for your area has been met. You also want to make sure that anything that required a permit did have one pulled for each aspect. If one was overlooked, it's best to get it now and just pay a penalty than to let it go on for months or even years. This could escalate into lawsuits or worse later. It is important that all your needs were met as to the standards and quality of the material and workmanship of your job. Always hold back about 10% of the contracted price for your final punch list. This will ensure that you will get your last items done, so they can receive the balance of pay from you. I know that I could have added so much more to listing what could be in a scope of work, but I feel that this will more than help you to get the best rehab for the lowest price.

SEAL THE DEAL WITH BEAUTIFUL CURB APPEAL

Curb appeal is one of the most important aspects of any real estate transaction. For me, it is the curb appeal that defines almost everything about my deal. How much will I offer? How much will it take to rehab the property? How does it compare to the surrounding living conditions?

Simply stated, if the curb appeal is not very good, I know that I can buy the property for a discounted price. And that's what my business is all about. Buying distressed homes and then raising the curb appeal through repairs to the property that not only raise curb appeal, but also the value too. Here are several ways that I use to bring up the value of houses to maximize my profit at resale.

The most important thing that I can do to improve curb appeal is to repaint the structure. A fresh new coat of paint adds value right from the start. Remember, you can only make a first impression once. Also, this will actually get you a higher appraisal than a house without a new paint job. You want to do the outside of an investment property first, and particularly the front. Getting the most noticeable portion in its best shape first will attract buyers immediately. You can't get a buyer to see the interior if they are not first pleased with the exterior. If the house is just dirty and the paint is in good shape, then a pressure washer can be used to clean up the exterior siding, gutters, downspouts, deck, fences and driveway. I even clean my roofs with one. Use the washer to remove any mold and mildew that can be seen on or near the house.

Pull your car in front of your property and take a hard look at what you see. This is going to be what your potential buyer see's too. If you see something that sticks out to you, fix it. Make sure there are no leaves piled up on the grass. Once you have disposed of any debris in the yard, make sure the lawn is mowed nicely. A fresh cut yard is a good sign that the rest of the home has been tended to correctly. Get rid of weeds and tools that are cluttering up any areas that can be seen from the street. Don't overlook windows or gutters that need to be cleaned. These are simple tasks that do not cost any money to perform, while adding a crisp clean appearance to the home. You may also want to remove any limbs touching the house or roof. This could scratch paint or cause roof leaks down the road. Another no-cost fix is to use a lawn edger around walkways, driveways and planter areas.

If your house may be looked at near dusk or dark, you want to make sure there is good light available. A decorative yard lamp could be added and this will help the appearance and also add security at the same time. Some people really like to line the driveway and walkway with little footlights. This adds great character to the house as well as a beautiful soft light shimmering as it leads people to your door. An inexpensive way to add light would be to add a fixture at your front door either overhead or a wall mounted light. These can be bought on any budget and the choice of styles is huge. While we are touching the topic of landscape, let me mention a few things. Landscape is where some people can make expensive mistakes. Since bushes, trees, and decorative plants can cost thousands in landscape design, you do not want to go overboard. Not even on your own home. Keep it simple and you can keep it cheap too. Around your mailbox post is a good place for some colorful flowers. You may also have some flowerbeds near your front entrance. This really looks good and can be done on a budget. Trim all the bushes to the same size and shape if they are in a group. This will make them look uniform as well as fancy. If I spend the money to plant any decorative trees, I get ones that will look decent all year round. Most of the trees that I would add would be fruit bearing trees or something that will bloom brilliantly during the year. Just don't blow your budget because you could make a mistake investing in landscaping that cost big dollars when for a few hundred, you can dress a yard up nicely. On a house I am doing this week, we trimmed back the bushes that had grown too high and then made a very nice design around them using decorative pine straw and wood chips. These items run about $3 a bale for the straw and about $5 a bag for decorative chips. It really dressed up the front of the house and I am sure will help me sell faster.

It's better to do a lot of little inexpensive things than it is to do one big expensive thing to add appeal. Dress up the front door with a nice color of paint that will go well with the house but add flair. It's just like dressing up an old suit with a new tie! Go a little further and add a fancy decorative doorknob and knocker set. Maybe even a brass kick plate. These items don't cost much but can add drama to the house. Keep in mind that if people don't like the outside of the house then they will probably never see the inside. You may not realize it, but bad curb appeal could be the reason that a house sits on the market for months.

One of the things that I saw that was great, happened as I was talking to my neighbor. She had been working on something in her yard for a couple of days so I wandered over to check it out. She had added a fountain in the front of her home and it was really pretty. Her and her husband bought a kit for the project for about $300. It had some nice stone structures and rocks that the water went through and they had dug out an area the plastic liner was placed into.

As the water trickled down the decorative stonework, the liner fit nicely into the ground and had some varieties of fish swimming in it. I thought this was a great addition, adding curb appeal and value, as well as a nice calming effect to sitting on the front porch in a rocker looking over the fountain. That was something else that I noticed. The charm of the front porch decorated with flowers, wind chimes and candles gave me the idea that I could dress up my houses for sale with this same décor to let a buyer feel that they could create the same charm if they bought my house.

If you have homes that have a lot of children living in the area as well as possible pet owners, you may want to make sure that if the house has a fence, that you make sure it is secure. On the house I have for sale now, we had to repair some areas of the fence. It's a six-foot tall wooden fence and we replaced some of the boards that had been knocked down or broken. This adds security to people with kids and pets.

Also, it would have been a deal killer for buyers to see the fence run down and tacky. We just put in a few new boards, sprayed it with bleach to clean it up and then put a good water sealer on it to make it last. We also did the same steps to the deck in the back to clean and preserve it. For a little over $100, we made two areas that may have driven a buyer away, look new and inviting again.

Let's summarize a few of the tips for making sure the curb appeal will seal the deal.

Pressure washing is a cheap way to clean up the entire exterior of any property.

Painting a fresh coat raises the value and appeal and is inexpensive.

No-cost items like cleaning windows, mowing lawns, raking leaves as well as trimming hedges, bushes, de-weeding and trimming branches from the house.

Lighting up your home with outside lights and fancy lamps and such.

Landscaping ideas that only cost a small amount for a huge difference.

Pond and fountains can be done to make a dramatic statement.

Repair fences and decks as well as using sealers to maintain a good look.

Make the place feel like home with front porch swings and rockers.

Decorate with flowers and candles…plant fruit bearing trees too.

There are hundreds of ways to add curb appeal…use your imagination!

SEVEN QUESTIONS TO ASK CONTRACTORS

1. How long have you been in business in this area? This is important because you want them to be established. In some cases, you may run into a company that is new and you will have trouble getting older references and such. If they have a good history in the area, you are less likely to have someone take your money and run. I like a 5 year history or more.

2. How many workers will be on the job daily? I want to make sure that there are enough bodies to do the job in a timely manner as well as not have half a crew on most occasions. If the job is small, it's ok to have a couple of workers only. On bigger jobs, I want manpower as we know time is money. Also make sure who you are dealing with will be on the job too. If they won't, they probably hired the work out to subs and are making money off you.

3. Are they licensed, bonded and insured? I do prefer that they have this in place however, I regularly hire small jobs that the individuals don't have it. In my SWAT system (secret ways and techniques) as well as my famous Rehab 101 system I have a 225 document forms CD. In this, I require all workers to sign my Waiver of Liability as well as my Lien Release form to protect myself against injury or property damage. Many times I will hire workers from new home construction sites to do "side work" for me. I know that if they work for a builder full time, they must have a license and insurance or they would not be hired by them.

4. Have they had any complaints locally or with the B.B.B. ? I will overlook a minor complaint or two provided that they have been resolved. When you file a complaint with the Better Business Bureau, they contact the party and give them the opportunity to make it right or work it out with the consumer and if worked out

there is no need for alarm. If they have multiples and they are long lasting and not resolved, I will not use them.

5. Will they supply you with 4 to 5 references? This is important because everyone will have 3 good references to give but sometimes these are friends or relatives and will say good things anyway. I want number 4 to be someone that they went back after being paid to fix a problem or touch up. This ensures integrity in the company or contractor that they stand behind their work. Number 5 is I ask them who their material suppliers are. I can call the paint store or material supply yard and ask them if they have had complaints there. Like if Sherwin Williams was a supplier, I would call and ask them about any complaints and also if they would recommend the contractor.

6. Can I use my contract or do they use their own? Once again, my 225 forms CD has all the contracts and such that it protects me as well as being fair to both sides. You want to spell out the pay schedule, such as paying as work is completed or "draws". This way you are not paying for work that is not done yet. Do you need to pay a material deposit? Use the term Balance Paid On Completion to make sure all work is done. Hold back 10% until a punch out list is completed to your satisfaction. Otherwise you may end up with an unfinished job.

7. Will you supply me a written warranty for labor and also a copy of the manufacturer's warranty from the materials? All materials such as paint, carpet, roofing and so on have written warranties on the labels or description. Make sure they will give you this info in writing as part of your contractual agreement so if anything goes wrong you are covered. Remember to put any and all details even if as an addendum to the contractor's paperwork no matter how petty it may sound. Your contract is your protection as well as the workers proof that they should be paid for their work. It works both ways so pay attention to detail.

SPRING FLINGS FOR YOUR PROPERTIES I

Part 1: Yearly Tasks to Cut Maintenance Costs on Your Investment and Personal Property

When the warmer weather starts to come around, it's time to get a few things going on around the house. The cold weather and elements have taken a season of toll on your roofs, decks, paint, landscape and flowers. I am putting together a series of articles that will drastically cut costs on your investment properties as well as your own. This article will help your painted exteriors last up to ten years or so, if you do this once a year.

Here are a few tips that I do to my properties when the sun comes out to play.

First, I pressure wash the outside of the house to get rid of dirt, mold and mildew. Starting with the roof, I stand on a ladder and spray chemical on the roof (bleach or a commercial cleaner). Do not spray chemicals on the roof when you are on the roof, you will slide off. After the roof dries, I can then get on it and rinse with water only from the washer. You can rent a pressure washer for about $65.00 a day. To save money, rent from a tool rental place on Saturday. Most rental places are closed on Sunday, so you actually get a free day because you don't have to return it till Monday morning. You may also split the cost with a neighbor for the rental. With an extra day, and a friend to split the cost with, you save double time.

Next, I pressure wash the gutters to get all the built up debris out. This will make your gutters last longer by removing all the wet muck that stays in even after someone cleans your gutters. After the gutters, start cleaning the siding and exterior surfaces of the house. I leave the bleach (or cleaner) on for about 10 minutes each side before rinsing with plain water. As you can tell, I am cleaning the house starting at the top and working my way down. Be careful spraying directly at the windows, as they may not be shut tight and water or cleaner could dip into the house.

Your next job is to wash the decks and rails. As long as you are about 12 inches away from a surface, you will only clean it, but if you want to remove flaking paint, you must get the pressure tip closer than 12 inches to remove flaking paint debris. When washing the decks, fences and steps, if the dirt build up is significant, I will use a medium pressure tip (40 degree) to sort of sweep the dirt off the surface. Then I will put in the highest-pressure tip (15 degree) and staying more than 12 inches from the surface, I will blast it clean. Doing the decks and fences tends to get a lot of wetness around and under the structures not only splashing bushes, but also the grass. Not to worry because your pressure washer automatically mixes the chemical and water at a 50/50 rate so it will harm small flowering plants, it will not hurt your grass or bushes at this diluted state.

The last items to be washed for great curb appeal and a neat appearance are the driveway and walkways of the property. The best way to do this is to use an attachment called a "hydra-scrub." Anyone who has ever cleaned a driveway the old fashioned way (with the regular wand of a pressure washer) knows that you clean about 6 inches by 3 feet at a time, taking hours, leaving streaks and causing a backache. But a nice white driveway looks great and is a great inexpensive improvement. The hydra-scrub attachment hooks up where the wand does, and is a 20-inch round object on handlebars and has a spinning action that cleans the driveway. It looks just like a floor buffer that the janitor uses to buff floors in buildings, schools and such. It does not use any chemicals, just water pressure. To get the driveway looking its best, clean it with the hydra-scrub to remove all the dirt from the porous concrete. It's just like mowing the grass. You walk slowly across the driveway cleaning a 20-inch wide area each pass. If you feel you are leaving streaks, then slow your pace down and the streaks will not appear. After I do the entire driveway, I then attach the wand back to the washer and use the chemical tip to saturate the driveway with cleaner or bleach. As before, the machine mixes a 50/50 content that will not harm the grass as it spills over the edge of the driveway. Now just let it evaporate and your driveway will become whiter and brighter as it dries.

This entire process can be done in just a few hours or a leisurely afternoon. The cost is under $100 with the rental of the washer, the hydra-scrub and the bleach or other cleaner used. I do this once a year to my properties and my paint jobs last almost twice as long…some 10 years or more. Now that's a good return on investment. Not only that, but my tenants see that I am taking care of the house, so they also seem to do more on their part too. Keep in mind that earlier I said to rent from a tool rental store on Saturday morning and you don't have to return the equipment till Monday morning. This only works at real tool rental places that close on Sundays. It does not work at the big hardware depots or chains, as they are open on Sundays.

I hope you got some great maintenance tips and money saving ideas from this article and watch REIP magazine for the continuation of this line of articles from me. Also, check into ordering some of the back issues of REIP mag as I have written many popular articles that people comment to me about as I speak around the country on my Rehab 101 system.

SPRING FLINGS FOR YOUR PROPERTIES II

Part 2: Cutting Maintenance Costs on Investment Properties and Home / Landscape 101 to Improve Appearance and Curb Appeal

This article is part 2 of a series I am putting together on lowering the maintenance costs for your investment properties as well as your own home. While often overlooked, the landscape has a very important role in your properties overall curb appeal. This can make or break a prospective buyer or tenant before they ever get out of the car to look at the home. Sure, I buy ugly houses, but I get a discount for it. You want to buy ugly and sell pretty houses to get the maximum profit on every deal. Here are a few things that I do to my properties that will add value, marketability and just improve the overall appearance of real estate.

Once a year, I will rent an aerator machine to use on the lawn. This machine can be walked behind as a self-propelled piece of equipment, or you can get the style that pulls behind a riding lawnmower. For do it yourselfers that are in good shape, I suggest the walk behind as you can get some exercise while doing the lawn. For all others, I recommend the type that pulls behind a riding lawn mower. The cost of rental is normally under $50 for the equipment. My favorite aerator is a pull behind that will pull plugs of dirt from the lawn as I ride around and usually cut the grass at the same time. These plugs that are being pulled are actually to add air (oxygen) to the soil aiding in the health and richness of my lawn and soil. Normally after the aerating part, you then overseed the yard. This means replenishing the newly plugged soil with fresh new grass seed that will fall into the holes and will provide a place to grow new grass. The purpose of this process once a year is to create a healthy, thick new grass lawn that really looks nice when maintained. If you are not the do it yourself type, this service can be hired out professionally for under $200 for an average lawn.

The next step is to make sure that your lawn has added chemical and such to make it a nice bright green color and to keep weeds, crabgrass and other unsightly vegetation out of your grass. A good fertilizer can be spread over the lawn with either a walk behind spreader or again with a riding lawnmower and attachment. That's how I like to do it. I normally will use the brand name (Scott's brand) with Halts added. The halts will stop any crabgrass growth and the fertilizer will stop weeds as well as unwanted growth of other plants.

After doing the above steps, my next one is to make sure that my lawn will remain green as it can be for as long as possible. For this, you will spread something over the lawn called (Lime). Lime is a product that will kill any forms of fungal growth or algae such as peat moss etc. this will keep your lawn nice in color and like I said before, if you only do this once a year, your lawn, tenants, buyers and renters will all be delighted with the beautiful results.

By adding half a dozen $30 bushes in front of the house for decoration is a great eye catcher. Make sure they are year round bushes so they don't lose their look at any season. Also, use mulch, wood chips or pine straw to bed around bushes, plant beds of flowers or in larger areas of trees to create a pro landscaped homes appearance.

Making sure to have the property groomed on a regular basis from here is the key to a good year long look for your property. Make sure the grass is cut regularly and that a weed eater has been used to groom around fences decks, trees and the mailbox. I also make sure that the lawn is done with an edger up and down the street curb, the driveway and walkways as well as any areas with sidewalks and such.

Last, make sure and add color to your lawns in areas that will catch someone's eye. Small flowers near the front door, around the mailbox and things like that are all good. Even hosta adds a pretty look for most areas. If you cut all the tree branches just above head level it will make the lawn look uniform as well as make it easy to mow the lawn. I hope these tips have added value to how you want to cut down on your maintenance cost on your investments. Please watch for my future tips and strategies for making thousands more rehabbing your investments.

SPRING FLINGS FOR YOUR PROPERTIES III

Part 3: More Tasks to Cut Maintenance Costs on Your Investment and Personal Property

This is part three and the final article on property maintenance. Many of the costs related to investment homes can be reduced greatly by preventative maintenance. By doing these steps on a regularly scheduled basis, you will be able to control the cost because you have time to shop around for bargains and get lots of bids, as opposed to having to hurry for e repair that has to be done right away, such as a leaky roof.

A periodic walk around the house can spot upcoming problems before they become emergencies to be fixed. You may see that the roof is starting to wear and get brittle. You may also notice gutters leaking or water stains forming around a skylight. These are the little things that can escalate to bigger problems. Here are some suggestions that may lead you in the right direction and save big bucks too.

You may not be as hands on as some people so you may want to hire someone to do the inspections for you. For those of you who know me and have some hands on experience, then you know I have inspection lists that I talk about in my seminars and you may use those, instead of hiring it out. Should you need to hire out the inspection, let me suggest that you seek a retired contractor or handyman. They do a great job and are just looking to make some extra money instead of being bored or watching TV. You can find these retired people by leaving flyers at Elks clubs, Veterans of Foreign wars (VFW) clubs, Kiwanis and other membership related groups that are generally retirees. My friend Nick Sidoti also reminded me that Bingo parlors are also a good place for retired workers.

Some of the most common areas to watch for besides roofs and gutters should be things like the chimney. How long has it been since it's been swept? Could this be a fire hazard? Is the flume guard open or shut? Not knowing this and starting a fire could cause smoke damage on the inside of a house.

You would also want to visually inspect the soffit and fascia (eaves) of the structure to see if any water damage or rot is starting to affect the area. How is the paint holding up on these areas? On brick houses, this is the only painted area besides doors and windows so don't overlook them. Take a good look at the siding of the property. Does it show signs of flaking paint or do you see physical damage to the surface, even if it is stucco or cinder block, it will still show symptoms if it is in need of repair.

As a contractor myself, I know that when we paint a property, we always paint all the way to the ground. So when I am inspecting the outside of a home, I look for the paint line to make sure it is all the way to the grass or ground. If there is an unpainted gap between the paint line and the ground then this indicates erosion of the soil. This is normally caused by water flow from rain and should be taken seriously. Water needs to be taken about 4 feet away from the side of the building to make sure that flooding or seepage does not occur. Believe me, you don't want water damage when you can definitely prevent it.

A common place for water rot is going to be in the thresholds below entrance doors. Check to see if these need to be replaced. You will stop water from entering your house with a cheap fix when replacing a bad threshold. Also, the bottoms of garage doors are subject to rot from rain. These bottom sections can run you about $150 each section to replace. I treat the bottoms of my garage doors with a good water sealer once a year to repel rain damage.

Get the water running away from your driveway by using add on pieces to your downspouts. Water can get underneath the concrete areas of driveways and walkways and cause them to crack and settle. It's also a good idea to cut limbs and bushes back from making contact with the sides of your house or roofs. This will allow water to be transferred to the house or will cause scraping and damage to your roof and siding.

Caulking around your door frames and window frames can help in lots of ways. One is keeping out water to keeping in the controlled air (heat and AC). Make sure that the framework around doors and windows are still square. It's hard to replace a door or window if you let the area get out of square.

I am not that good at electrical, so once a year I have someone come and check the panel for rust and moisture. They also look for any signs of burned wires or loose connections. I can request that they actually label the breakers so I know what controls what. You should get your heating and AC checked at the same time. Filters in these items need to be changed or cleaned in order to run at peak performance. Getting your lint tube from your clothes dryer is a great thing to do to cut down on dryer time for your clothes. It could make a 10-minute or more difference to how fast your clothes dry. Water heaters and furnaces will also need to be inspected and fine tuned for best results.

Once a year or more I will check the property over for signs of pests. This could be birds, raccoons, squirrels, roof rats, termites or whatever. Animals can cause big holes as well as big damage to houses if not fixed right away. If you think an animal has entered your home, bang loudly with trashcans or on the siding to drive them out before you cover the hole. To trap and animal inside normally means it will pass away inside and the smell will enter the house. You can rid the house of animal and pet odors with one of these 2 products. One is called ODORXIT and the other is called ODOBAN. You can do a google search to find these items near you. One more thing is to make sure to test all the smoke detectors in your houses. It could save your life.

Well, I hope this 3 part series on cutting maintenance costs to your investment properties and home has been helpful. Anytime you can cut cost by doing a little preventative action, it will benefit you in the long run. Please look for my future writings coming soon.

SWAT – SECRET WAYS AND TECHNIQUES

Over the years, investors and homeowners have read and studied my Rehab 101 System and had great success remodeling for a fraction of general contractor costs. After all, saving thousands of $$$'s is great in any situation. More and more people are coming to me at seminars and my live trainings and asking if there was a way that I could put together a visual hands on training showing exactly what to do, how to do it, what products to use, how much will it cost and where do I get it?.

I was positively on fire for the this because I had been filming several recent rehabs on properties that had not been covered in most any other fix up shows or trainings anywhere. Even though I give seminars and trainings all over the country and have for over 2 decades, I still watch and learn from other speakers and have found that a lot of them will TELL YOU WHAT THEY DID TO MAKE MONEY, BUT NOT TELL YOU HOW THEY DID IT! Therefore you leave the training thinking you know what to do just to find you were just as confused as to what to do as you were before you saw them.

This is the reason why I created the SWAT system for real estate. It is Secret Ways And Techniques (SWAT) to rehab property all on DVD's so you can watch every detail. I also included material and labor cost prices as well as over 200 forms to use for liability waivers, making offers, contracts, deeds and all else you need.

In a nutshell, I combined what was going to be a seven (7) course series offering each one individually for a nominal price each. After conducting a test of these products with people who had my Rehab 101 system, the suggested that I combine all seven courses into one TOTAL COVER IT ALL SYSTEM. After much thought, I decided they were right. Make a system that is Like no other and covers more than any other Rehab system and do it For A Fraction Of The Cost Of Others! I designed the perfect way to teach fixing up real estate no matter if you have never done a deal before or whether you have done 100 deals and are an expert. Here is a brief description of what I created.

My son James and some of his college buddies wanted to buy a house, fix it up to live in and sell it in three years for a profit. They had never done a deal or done any remodeling in their lives before. After securing a great deal, I took them and taught them how to remodel the house and in about 8 days created over 100K in equity. I put all the training on DVD's for this project. Among other things we pulled carpet and pad finding old hardwood flooring. By me showing them how to rent equipment and sand and re-stain the hardwoods, we saved 10k on this alone. I made 5 DVD's on fixers for fortunes that included me teaching wallpaper removal, sheetrock repair, and pressure washing the decks and exterior.

Another portion that saved literally $1500 or more was when I showed them how to strip and re-finish the cabinets. We cut a hole in a wall and put in double French doors and put tile in the kitchen in some areas and then matched the wall paint colors to the tile. I demonstrated how to put in a drop ceiling and install a floating hardwood simulated floor in the basement so they could rent that portion of the house out and make cash flow. By doing the painting and unskilled labor it was easy to show them how to create big profits on any real estate rehab.

Also in SWAT, my friend Carl Fischer took over a property in Wisconsin. After 2 years of trying to sell the house, we decided to film what to do to this house to make it sell. He had estimates for a new roof, new countertops, new appliances and total bathroom remodeling. It also needed general curb appeal help and the cost was close to 20k. By using more of my latest Swat secrets, we refinished the countertops without replacing them (yes there is a $30 product for that). We got the roof replaced for less than ½ the original estimate, replaced the garage doors and totally gave the fence and yard a brand new look. The entire process was captured on 2 DVD's called Rehab in Action and was done for about 7k in repairs. With paint and carpet and a few little secrets on curb appeal, Carl's house sold in 3 days for a $40,000 profit WHEW!!!

I have always stood by the promise that when I teach rehabbing, I tell you what product to use, show it to you, demonstrate how it works, tell you how much it costs and tell you what aisle to get it and what store. SWAT is no exception. I made a TOOLS DVD to show you everything you need for any rehab, big or small. You can buy this collection of tools one at a time or get them all at once. They range from $3 to about $30 and most hardware stores will carry them all. Tape maskers for painting, circuit analyzers for wiring diagnostics, hole repair patches, moisture meters and so on. This is invaluable to any rehabber…and after all, we are all rehabbers when it comes down to real estate.

As some of you know, I am an accredited teacher on EPA courses such as Mold inspection and Lead based paint rules and regulations. I have had classes on each of these filmed and turned to DVD format to inform you of your limits and responsibilities for both. Did you know that proving mold exists in a bank owned REO that you could qualify for big discounts saving up to 25% or more on the selling price? Or did you know that if you do not know the rules for remodeling a property built before 1978 could get you fines of up to $37,500 per violation. These DVD's will provide you what you need to know.

Trying to give a full description of the SWAT system would take hours and page after page, but let me say this. There are 17 DVD's and 3 CD's and it can be in full DVD and CD format like most training courses, or I have made it 100% digital by putting it on a flash pack (8 gig usb drive) to save you money. The CD's are 225 forms, waivers, offer makers, deeds, assignments and all other forms needed to do real estate in any capacity. It also has an offer making CD so you look like a pro when you submit an offer and a CD with all the material and labor costs that contractors use for estimating. This is a total of 18 HOURS live training!!! With all this at your fingertips, you will make far better decisions as well as profits in your real estate careers by having SWAT. If you are brand new to investing or a seasoned pro, check out the SWAT SYSTEM. There has never been a rehab training anywhere even close to the quality of this one at any cost. I look forward to being a part of your success. Pete Youngs AKA Mr. Rehab.

TERMITES CAN EAT YOUR HOUSE, AND YOUR PROFITS

One of the biggest scares homeowners and real estate investors face is the possibility of a property having termites. Sure, you can get a termite inspection to tell you if you have them, but for most of us, once we know about the termites, it's too late and the damage has already started.

That's why in my SWAT System, I teach people how to determine if the property has termites, once had termites, and to tell if you are in danger of attracting termites down the road. The following info is taken from my termite inspection forms and should be a real help to those who want to know a.s.a.p. the real deal about detecting termites.

As always when inspecting a house, I dress in protective clothing (jeans and a t- shirt) or something I won't mind getting a little dirt on. Then I get a stepladder, a screwdriver for poking and prodding, a light for dark areas and something to jot my notes and finds on.

You should then look in places that attract termites such as where any wooden part of the house touches the ground. This could be siding, trimwork, mailbox post etc. areas that seem wet all the time or portions of your yard that stay damp a lot is also suspect when near your house or other wooden structures. You should look at your cinder block areas for deterioration of foundation structure, or any major cracks in the mortar or brick areas.

Termites sometimes make mud tunnels to live in. look for these tunnels throughout your inspection. They will look similar to what some of us know as dirt dobber (type of bee) tunnels. Check all wood surfaces that are exposed in your garages, carports, under house storage area and basements. Screen porches that have a dirt floor should have several inches between the floor and wood surfaces. Check any other structures that may be attached to your house.

Another overlooked item are planter boxes and potted plants in wooden fixtures. When watered regularly, the moist dirt and wood become a favorite place for termites to try to establish squatter's rights on your house. Keep in mind that paper is a wood product and wet…is just as much an attractant to termites as a rotted 2x4.if porch or deck steps are wooden and tough the ground directly you need to check here. Poke and prod at the wood closest to the dirt looking for soft wood that your screwdriver easily tears through, as well as slight tunnels in the wood. Always put some sort of concrete pad or decorative rock under steps where they meet the ground. Moist heat surrounds your furnace, so check well around this area.

Termites stay where the food is. Some areas that attract termites are old stumps from cut down trees. Your firewood pile is another if it gets wet or stays uncovered. Decks are prime candidates as well as fences as they tend to touch the ground and have sunken posts in the dirt for support. Wooden landscape ties and mulch flower beds draw termites also.

Other areas that provide a wet environment will be suspect for termites too. Downspouts, outside water hoses, leaky sinks and toilets, air conditioners and sewer lines or where water runoff is around the house should be checked periodically.

To summarize what you should do to get the skinny on termites you should do these things when thinking of buying as an investment or to check your own home about every six months.

Look closely at the entire exterior of the house and any structure connected to it for mud tunnels coming from the ground climbing up the house…and nearby trees. Remember that plumbing leaks from kitchen and bath areas should be checked too. Window frames, window sills, thresholds and siding should be poked with a screwdriver looking for soft wet wood or slight tunnels that indicate termite infestation. Remember any plants in big wooden containers or planter boxes outside your window are common to find trouble. Any wood from porches, siding trim or decks and fences that touch the dirt should not be overlooked. If you have a crawl space, use a flashlight and check it out. Get on your stepladder and check where the foundation meets wood for the first time. This is a common area. Wooden decks and such near swimming pools are an attractant for the little beasts. Attics should be inspected on the beams, decking and structure for mud tunnels as well as little (sawdust anthills) as that's what they look like. Though if you have a sawdust mound that has a hole as round as a pencil, don't panic…these are more commonly done by carpenter bees and are not as scary as termites. Some termites fly. When looking keep an eye out for wings that have been shed by these types.

And most important…Write down what you find to show exterminators if need be.

THEFT PROOF REHABBING

One of the most common things I run across no matter where in the country our properties may be, is theft or vandalism. I don't know any investor that has not faced this as sad as that may be. It doesn't always have to be serious, but it is always inconvenient. From neighborhood kids tagging with spray paint to full blown breaking entering and burglary, you want to avoid this if possible. Here are my suggestions.

My first and favorite tip is to use regular car wax, yes the car wax that you use on your car, to make the windows where you can't see in. It doesn't matter if you use Turtle wax from a tin can or Simonize from a squeeze bottle. All you do is take a sponge or rag and cover it with the wax, then wipe the glass windows totally to cover. When the wax dries, you will not be able to see inside the building. I do all the lower windows including the garage door windows. This way no one can see any tools, materials, ladders, paint and such that someone may want to steal.

The benefits of using wax are that it covers lots of area inexpensively. Compared to installing an alarm system or hiring a security guard, this repels most unwanted visitors for literally under $10. No window shades or curtains are needed during fix up and clan up is a breeze. Just wipe windows down with dry cloths and it comes right off, fast!! It also reduces fog and condensation on the glass. Cool Right?? The best part is that your workers can spray, brush or roll paint and the windows come squeaky clean with no overspray or even scraping the paint of the window panes after even brushing them.

You also want to keep the place looking as if someone is there at the house on a regular basis. This can be as simple as keeping newspapers and advertising swag picked up from driveways, doorknobs and keeping the mailbox empty. Move things around. If there is not a trash can out front, put one there. Move it from one spot to another regularly. Talk to the next door neighbors and let them know who you are and give a contact number for you in case they see something unusual, or especially people working when you're not expecting work, such as late night, Got it?

Keep the grounds up by making sure the grass is cut. This is the most obvious thing that a house is vacant (tall grass, unkept yard) and will attract unwanted visitors. Open the upper story windows occasionally on the front of the house so it can be seen from the street. No one can see in the upper windows, but it does show signs of people being at the house regularly.

Never Leave ladders and such on the outside of the house. Ladders give someone the option to see inside upper windows (unless you waxed them like I said). Never leave empty 5 gallon buckets around the outside as we use them like a small step ladder to gain access. Always keep paint cans and buckets inside the locked house. Vandals the find paint outside can splash the paint all over the house, garages and driveway causing havoc to your property.

As far as tools and materials are concerned, you should protect them the best you can. No one knows better than me that after 30 years in the rehabbing business, I hate moving all my stuff on every job. So what I do is make a safe place for my expensive tools and equipment and leave my easily replaceable things out. This way if a thief gets in, they may settle for the "low hanging fruit" for a quick in and out without searching out my more expensive tools and such. I may lock up all my power tools in something referred to as a "Gang Box". It's like a big tool box on wheels that locks up tight and is hard to break into. A gang box is also quite large and heavy meaning when it is full, you can't lift it to put it in a truck with even two or three people. Therefore they will have to make some serios noise trying to break into it and will normally be more risk of getting caught than robbers want to take.

As far as paint sprayers and pressure washers that you can't put in a gang box, this is what I do. I find a good sized closet in the garage or a bedroom to roll my bigger items and paints. Remember the widows are waxed so you can't see in, but once I put my bigger items in the closet, I put a keyed doorlock and a deadbolt lock on the door making it a lot of trouble to get in. Plus the fact that you can't see what's in there, you might not risk going in. Remember, an ounce of prevention is worth a pound of cure. You may choose to do this to a whole bedroom or downstairs area in the property if you need the space to store. Most people don't know this so I will tell you. When you are putting in hardwood floors, you need to store the uninstalled flooring in the property for 5 to 7 days so the wood acclimates itself to the climate of where it will be installed. NOT doing this will cause your floors to shrink after installation and leave cracks, gaps and imperfections. If your installer does not tell you this, TELL them. This is important to do. A locked room will stop your flooring from being stolen during acclamation process.

The above is just a few of the many recommendations I make in my live trainings as well as in my S.W.A.T. training systems and Rehab 101.

THINGS THAT MAKE YOU GO HMMM!

In my latest deal that closed on Friday, there were many things that happened from the inspection that most of the people doing rehabs might have overlooked. Part of my teaching style in my systems and live events are to teach you things that you would not have realized on your own.

Sometimes you must look very hard a property to find the little things that will add up, and cost you thousands of dollars that you had not intended to spend. I teach how to do property inspections…one of the most important tasks that will save you big bucks, if you know what to look for. See, the buyer will hire a property inspector to list the defects of your property as a tool for getting a discount on the deal, or get you the seller, to pay for these repairs. Here's what we had to recognize on my last deal.

First, the gutters did not have a nice line to them. They had sagging areas that made the property look as if it would be best to replace the gutters. This would have cost around $800.00 to do. But for under $20.00, I got some gutter brackets that attached with a screw gun, and had a helper use a 2 x 4 stud to push up on the gutters to get them back in line as I screwed the brackets tightly into the fascia board. This made the appearance 100% better and saved about $780.00.

Next problem was something that most would have missed seeing, unless you have a trained eye. There had been some siding replaced due to moisture rot on the bottom of the house around the entire exterior. (Probably from the gutter situation). An inspector would have picked up on this and made a big deal out of it. You see, siding must not touch the ground around the house. This makes for easy insect infestation such as termites, and also stops some loan institutions from financing a deal with this situation. Commonly, siding must be about 6 inches from the ground to be considered correct. To save money, we did not tear out the siding and start over. We got on both ends of the side portions of the house and measured up six inches from the ground, and then snapped a chalk line that marked the siding all the way across each side of the house. Then we adjusted the blade on our skill saw to ½ inch and used it to trim the bottom six inches off the house. This now was acceptable when an inspection would be done.

The toilets in the house seemed as if they could be kept if they were given new working parts on the inside. I put newspaper around the bottoms and flushed a few times, then left the newspaper overnight. When we returned the next day, we found that the paper had absorbed some water. This indicated that the wax ring in both toilets had been seeping a little. So by the time you have added up the moving parts

Or guts to be replaced, then the wax rings and then the plumbers labor cost per hour it was actually cheaper to just buy new toilets. The new ones came complete with all new parts, most installed already. Therefore, it takes the plumber less time at his hourly rate to install new toilets rather than rebuild the old ones. It also looks good to the buyer to see brand new fixtures.

The cabinets were stained dark brown and had a thin layer of poly on them. They really needed a fresh look to avoid replacing them. I have written techniques on how to prep and paint stained cabinets to a nice white look but here; this is a great way to restore a brand new look for under $5.00. There is a product in most any store that sell cleaning supplies called "Old English Scratch Remover". You pour this dark oil onto a white terry cloth rag and rub over the entire cabinet area. This will not only blend in any light and dark areas, but also give the appearance of freshly stained and varnished cabinets. Saving easily about $1000.00 this one tip is one you will use over and over in your investing career.

Last, was the big killer. If overlooked this could easily cost you several thousand dollars and in many cases is a deal breaker if you do not replace it. It is also something you should use as a discount when buying the house as an investor.

Either way, somebody is likely to have to pay for this replacement. I am talking about polybutylene water piping. Usually identified by being blue in color, this pipe has a reputation of breaking and leaking causing thousands in water damage. Though many houses may have it, nobody wants it. Not only is it unpopular, it's expensive to replace. But using the techniques I teach in Rehab 101 we got our estimate to replace the entire pipe in the house and the underground service from the street down from $7995.00 to about half the cost at $4200.00. That's a great savings on just that item alone. So be careful not to overlook a house's "fine print" when you do your initial walk around. See beyond what you think you see, and learn to look for the less obvious repairs that could make or break a good deal.

TIPS TO SELL HOUSES FAST

In the present market, properties are taking longer to sell and are being sold for less than the asking price. Here are some tips to help speed up the market time on houses.

The first thing that needs your attention is the yard and landscape. You must make sure that the grass is freshly mowed and looking healthy. Putting powdered lime on the grass will make it nice and green. All the tree branches should be cut at head level to look uniform and allow for easy mowing around them. Using colorful annual plants really sharpen up the place and red seems to be the most used color of flowers.

I always pressure wash houses no matter what condition they are in. This removes unwanted dirt and pollen, removes mold and can clean up dirty looking roofs as well. With a Hydra- Scrub attachment you can clean the driveway and all walkways leading to the house. You can also clean carport floors and such with this great attachment. No one wants to buy a home that has cobwebs and such around the front entrance. Make sure to have the front entrance looking its best. Remember, if the outside of the house does not impress people, they may never even see the inside.

Make sure that you put a new paint job on the house. If you are selling, this will improve the value as well as the appearance of the property. If renting, I may not repaint the outside if it cleans up well with a pressure washer. If you paint a rental house, you may hurt your positive cash flow earnings. Think of this; a paint job could run you about $2400.00 If you only make $200.00 a month positive cash flow and your tenant wants a 12 month lease, you just made your profit go down to zero for the whole year and that is bad. If you paint a rental house, get a two-year lease, that way you will at least make $100.00 a month positive cash flow.

The front door of the house is such an important feature. It is like a tie on a great suit. The suit can stay the same but you can get many different looks by just changing the tie. The same goes for the front door of a house. You can dramatically change the look of the house by using a fire engine red door or something that really grabs attention. This is a low cost tip that will be worth the time and effort.

Another good tip is to make sure the windows are clean. It does not take much to clean the windows and if you can't be bothered to do it, hire someone who will. This does not cost much, but if you overlook it, you may turn away a good prospect from the house. While checking the windows for easy opening and closing, take a close look at the shutters. Do they need a coat of paint? Are they installed right side up?

Keep an eye out for the little things and you will speed up the selling process.

Advertising is another key element to selling a house fast. You need to have many signs directing people to your property. If you just put a sign in the yard, the only people who know the house is for sale already live in the neighborhood. You may even want to hire one of those flat fee services that list your house and put it on the internet. You may consider putting it on E-BAY or CRAIGSLIST to attract out of town buyers. I also use a coded lockbox on the doorknob that holds the key to the house. Some people would like to look at the house without someone there who may be pushing high-pressure sales as they look around. Think of how many times you have made an appointment to show the house and the people never turn up and you have wasted your time. I give them the code and allow them to view the house and then call me to let me know what they thought of the house. Also, let the neighbors know you are selling, and talk to them about the benefits of the house. The buyers may contact people in the area and ask them about the house.

Always try to have some sort of incentive for the people to buy. If you give a $2000.00 carpet allowance or such, it appears that you are giving the buyer a discount or the chance to choose a piece of the house that is personal to them.

Maybe even letting them choose wallpaper for the kitchen. I just want them to feel like they are able to make something about the house seem like theirs.

Most importantly is to really think about the price you are asking for the property. Try to stay away from the retail prices. Right now, the retail real estate market is down. But that is o.k. with us as investors. We don't buy retail real estate or sell retail. We buy properties below market value and should sell below market value to allow for a faster sale. Since I am a general contractor turned investor, I use my techniques in my Rehab 101 system to actually create a profit while I do the rehab. If you can cut the cost of fixing up a property by 50%, then you have actually added that much in profit back into the sale of the house. Be smart about hiring lower cost contractors and take advantage of contractor discounts and such. Remember, if you cut the rehab cost by $10,000.00 you just created an additional ten grand to your bottom line profit.

TOP 10 RENOVATIONS TO ADD VALUE

Recent trends show that home renovation is sweeping the country today. With homeowners and investors alike, this business has become one of the most popular trends this decade. There are many people out there who are confused about what to do and what not to do. Surely, making a part of the home look better is always a plus. However, you can spend a lot of money on renovations that merely make the house prettier and more marketable, but do not actually raise the value of the home. I have had years of experience renovating hundreds of homes and have seen people waste thousands of dollars fixing up houses for resale and can't get the money they spent on rehab back out of the property when they sell. If you are going to sink a substantial amount of money in a property, make sure it is something that will add value to the structure.

For example, the kitchen is the top one thing that will add value to your deal. More than other renovations, the kitchen has far more of a payback value for the money spent…when you sell. Everybody loves a clean, modern kitchen that has all the latest amenities. A common renovation includes a new stove and oven. It should also include an island piece for prep and serving. New countertops and upgraded cabinets are great too. For big savings on refinishing cabinets, refer back to a recent issue of REIP magazine for my article on GIVING KITCHENS AND BATHROOMS AN INEXPENSIVE FACELIFT.

The second best rehab job as far as paying you back when you sell is the bathrooms. A new toilet, sink and vanity freshen up old bathrooms quite nicely. Don't forget new flooring and possibly upgrade the tub to a bigger size garden tub. Replace shower curtains with sliding glass doors to add value and appeal. Make sure you have a nice linen storage with plenty of room for towels and accessories. Use soft neutral colors so that it will go with almost any decorating taste.

Interior painting, carpet and décor will bring up resale value faster than water drains downhill. As a relatively inexpensive facelift, paint and carpet are one of the first things that catches a buyer's eye. We all know that spouses and partners in the business are keen to the fact that properties are more appealing with fresh clean walls and floors. Adding a little chair rail or some crown molding really accents a room without costing you the farm. And once again, this adds value!!!

Exterior painting to re sell a property is a must. If you have seen my seminars, you will remember me saying that on rentals and lease options, I pressure clean the outside to see if it looks pretty good with just a good cleaning. I don't just automatically paint it because that is how others have done it. See, If I am selling outright, there will be someone getting an appraisal on the house. Therefore, I will paint it because it adds value to the appraisal, but if I automatically paint my rental exterior, it does not add monetary value to what I get from my renter or lease op buyer. Instead I will leave the exterior painting for those situations up for a negotiating factor I can use to manipulate the terms or down payment of the clients. See the difference of the added value?

Next are window and door upgrades. This will add value and appeal to almost any home. To get a new look but also save money, leave the frames of the doors (jams) and buy door blanks. Add the new doorknobs and hinges and paint all doors and jams to match. A door blank is much less expensive than a pre-hung door. Also, look into windows that offer savings in heating and air conditioning bills. Over time, in the savings they create in utilities they may just pay for themselves.

Flooring of any kind when it's new will make most any room look better. Never put carpet in bathrooms or areas they may become wet on a regular basis. A better way to go would be linoleum or tile for these areas. Then decorate with throw rugs that can be removed and washed.

When doing carpets, don't overspend as most people do. As I teach in my training camps across the U.S. most people make the mistake of buying a great carpet and a cheap pad. This is exactly opposite of what you want. You want a great pad and you can lessen the quality and cost of the carpet. To get many years of great wear and being able to stand up to cleaning, you should use a 6 to 8 pound pad made of multi-colored specs and cover it with 40 ounce carpet. This is a very nice combination for rental houses and properties you are fixing up for sale.

Room additions are next in line for adding value. Most beneficial if it is added on the main floor, any room addition adds living space and square footage to the home. It can be a Study, office, extra bedroom, adding a bathroom and so forth. Anytime you can add useable space to a property, you are adding value.

Adding a fireplace such as in a den or living room is a popular choice from some of the research I did for this article. As many of you may have noticed, it is not uncommon to see fireplaces in the bedrooms of most new high end homes. Not only does it add a decorative flair, but it's cozy, romantic, inviting and even warm. Though you may not want to add some additions to you house, pick and choose the one or a few that would work in you situation and use it to raise not only the value, but also the profit figure on the bottom line when you sell.

Renovating the unfinished basement is one of my favorites. Just think how much more appealing a house would be if all that space downstairs was suddenly useable living area. And talk about adding value…The sky is the limit. Think about what someone could do with this space. Well, let's see. You could move the teenage kids downstairs. You could add bedrooms to the area and a kitchen and have a rental area. It could be an In Law suite. You could turn it into a home theater or you could make it a game room or you could use it as a home office and run a business out of it. You could practically interest a buyer in most of those possibilities listed above, but for Pete's sake, if you have an unfinished basement...finish it!

The last of these 10 renovations would be the Heating and Air conditioning units of the property. This is where the heat hits the fan! By upgrading and old HVAC setup in a house, you have literally relieved someone's fear that the unit will fail and need replacing. What's the most common thing we investors do when selling a house now? We buy a home warranty for a year and offer it with the house so if something goes out in the form of a furnace or A/C unit, then it's covered and the buyers are more comfortable with that. To help make the decision on how to handle buying a new heating system or A/C unit.

Keep this in mind. The life of a furnace or air unit is about 15 to 17 years on most brand name makers. There is a tag on heat, a/c units and water heaters that tell what year they were made. Seek out this tag and you'll have a pretty good idea how much longer the unit has before you can expect a problem. I hope that this information will shed some light on what renovations will I actually get value out of doing them, as opposed to ones that look pretty, but cost you profit and time, with not much benefit. Mr. Rehab says, "buy smart, buy many, and ...

TOXIC TERRORS THAT AFFECT HOMES

MOLD:

Mold in houses has become one of the most popular scares in recent years. Although it has been around since before caveman days, our industry is always out to find something new to charge thousands of dollars to correct. Most molds, even black in color are not the toxic poison type of mold that causes illness in people. The temporary fix is to use a 50/50 mix of bleach and water to clean the surface. This does not kill the mold, it just removes the surface visibility and unless you take away the moisture or cause of the mold it will return. For mold remediation of black mold and mold infestation, please refer to my article on mold in your previous issues of REIP magazine. If you have significant mold in sight, one of the brands of product I recommend is Microban. It is highly effective in handling problems associated with mold, fungi, bacteria, germs and so on. You may find it by calling a janitorial supply company from your yellow pages book.

Microban is used by professionals for mold remediation; yes the toxic black mold remediation that costs thousands of dollars by people wearing HAZMAT suits. It is also used for water damage, flooding, sewage backups and such. Another type of product for the same problems is called Shockwave and may be easier to find locally. The effects of mold can be breathing problems such as asthma, headaches, rashes, stomach ailments and so on. The four steps to eliminating mold are to contain it, kill it, remove the dead mold, and protect from further contamination. This may mean an exhaust fan in bathrooms, better ventilation in rooms and crawl spaces. Placing dehumidifiers in strategic areas in the house, or using hepa filter air cleaners as well. You can get a mold test kit at major hardware stores for about $10.

LEAD BASED PAINT:

Lead based paint is a toxin found in many living quarters and can cause serious illness or even death. It is especially toxic to children and can even affect babies before they are born. A good thing is that lead based paint that is not deteriorating is not a threat. Also there are options to be done to reduce and eliminate the hazard. You can contact lead from paint by breathing it, touching flaking areas of paint, dusty paint surfaces and during renovations it can be cast into the air from hammering, sanding, sweeping and more. Youngsters can get it on their hands from doors, windowsills floors and such and then put their hands in their mouths as we commonly see them do. This can affect brain function as well as nervous systems in children. Long-term exposure leads to hearing problems, learning problems, behavior problems, headaches and lots more. Adult symptoms are more described as reproductive problems in both genders. Difficulties during pregnancy, a rise in blood pressure, nerve problems as well as bad digestion, memory loss and muscle pain. This threat goes lower risk in younger houses because lead paint was stopped for making and using it around 1978. So newer houses have less risk of this problem. Lead based paint test kits are available at most larger hardware stores for about $4 a kit. The most common places to check would be windows and sills, doors and doorframes, stairs, railings, decks, screen porches and let's not forget furniture. Don't overlook your prized antiques either. If it's old furniture that has original finished surfaces, this area is often overlooked. Any peeling, flaking or chipping paint accompanied by dust is suspect. To do it yourself or hire a pro for lead abatement, you need to stay clear of sanding, sweeping and vacuuming as this will spread the dust air born. Lead based paint must be removed (the painted structure) or most common is to encapsulate the paint. Products can be bought that you spray, brush or roll over the lead paint to seal in the hazard. The E.P.A. (where some of my research was obtained) has a booklet for free on lead based paints; it's effects, the abatement and prevention available upon your request. This will provide you with some useful info.

METH LABS:

Another toxic terror that is becoming more well known is finding out that the house you bought or are thinking of buying as an investment was once used as a meth lab, a crack house, or some other form of drug related house. This came up at a seminar I am giving in Portland this week. The person asked my opinion about his deal and that it was previously a crack house. He made an offer and it was accepted. The house, he said, was a property seized by law enforcement and it had been vacant for a while. I listened and told him that I would not want to buy this house myself. Puzzled, he asked why. First, this information will need to be disclosed to all interested in buying it and could be a turn off. Second, I asked how it had been (cleaned up). He told me that the city had given the house a clean bill of health. So I said will they accept any liability if anyone has any health related problems? He said no. I told him that all liability would rest on his shoulders and he would be solely responsible for possible trouble. He thanked me, and said he really wanted to be talked out of the deal because it was too much for him to do on his first deal. It was almost a total gut job. Now keep in mind, under his circumstances, I told him no I wouldn't but it myself. However, I do know several investors with a lot more experience in this type of house that would have jumped all over this deal, and made a huge profit as well. It was the experience level here. He probably should get his feet wet without starting with an issue on the house like that one. The problem with drug related houses is that there is no set way to tell how much residue is still in the cracks, crevices, vents, gaps and other areas that may still cause exposure to the toxins. There is no real data on how long of exposure to this will it then affect someone. It is the responsibility of the homeowner from purchase on for any liability caused by this. So how do you know if it's a drug house or meth lab? Generally there are beakers and burners and test tubes present shortly after abandoned. There may be a smell present and cans of cooking fuels around. There may be burn marks on countertops as well as dusty residue in kitchen and bathroom areas. Samples can be taken by taking scotch tape and (lifting) debris from surfaces of countertops, sinks, carpets, bedding, curtains, floors and utensils found in the property. Have them analyzed by a law agency and get a report. Then decide if you want to do the deal. Remember, this does not scare a seasoned investor who knows how to deal with creative real estate. This is an opportunity, or a niche, because most people will pass on these kind of deals, and the ones that do them…PROFIT.

CARBON MONOXIDE:

This is a problem that can be found in many homes. Even mine. I just recently had my furnace replaced and was about to remodel my basement and add some on to the house when I noticed an exhaust pipe from the furnace had separated from a portion of pipe. This had been easily 3 months or so since the job was done. I went to a local hardware store and got a test kit for about $6 and did the test. It came back as a dangerous reading from the kit. If not found, this could have turned out to be serious health risk. CM is an odorless, colorless gas or liquid and is hard to detect without a test kit. Though my culprit was a furnace, others could include kerosene and gas space heaters, leaking chimneys, gas water heaters, wood stoves, and gas operated equipment like cars. Some people in winter will start their cars in the garage to let them warm up before leaving for work and even with the door open this poses a threat. Even in low concentrations, fatigue and chest pains can happen. With more exposure it may cause dizziness, lack of vision or concentration, headaches and nausea. Exposure can be fatal. To reduce risks EPA guidelines say to keep appliances properly adjusted. Always use vented heaters and never use alternate fuel sources on thing meant for a certain kind of fuel. Such as do not use gas in a kerosene heater. I have seen workers do this on jobsites in the cold. You need to have an exhaust fan over gas stoves. Never grill indoors with any gas driven bar b que and have your furnace checked and serviced often. I hope this information will help and educate you as to the dangers of TOXIC TERRORS IN YOUR HOME.

WINTERIZING YOUR HOME

Old man winter has reared his ugly head as we are now headed for cold weather. After concentrating on hurricanes and rainstorms, we now have the chore of prepping our homes and investment properties from cold weather related problems. Here's a few suggestions to make the winter a little easier for us all.

First, make sure that the insulation in your attic is sufficient for your area. If it seems lacking in depth or amount, a cheap fix is blown in insulation. This covers well, keeps in the heat and is done very fast. Many companies that do this are listed in the yellow pages or business section of the phone book. Also, the pink stuff (in rolls) is equally effective for your attic. All exterior walls should have insulation, so when you are doing rehabs or adding to a house, make sure you insulate any outer walls.

Next is caulking. Use a good quality latex and silicone combo caulk such as White Lightning brand or Dap Alex. These are 25 to 40 year caulks with low price and water clean up. Check all areas around the house for a good and proper caulking job. Anywhere that has damaged caulk or is in need of some is one of the most common areas we lose heat and a/c and our bills skyrocket. You will want to caulk around all doors, windows, cornerboards, siding, vents and such. Cracks in siding should be done as well as entry areas on the house such as water spigots and where electrical wires come into the house. Exhaust vents for fans and clothes dryers too. It's also a good idea to get those Styrofoam covers that connect on to your outside water spigots to protect from freezing temps leading to busted water pipes. For just pennies per foot, you can buy foam insulation for your exposed water pipes in your basement or garage (the most common places for busted water pipes from freezing).

Weather stripping around doors and windows can rob you from heat as well. Most hardware stores can sell you rolls of weatherstripping and it's easily installed by any "do it yourselfer". As far as this area goes, don't forget the part under your doors on the threshold. This area is almost always forgotten and usually needs replacing the most. Open all your entrance doors and check the threshold for wear and tear. You'll be glad you did. For those pesky drafts that get through the window sills and under doorways, you can buy or make what we call a draft snake, These are just round fabrics filled with whatever you want and made to the size of the bottoms of doors and window sill. This keeps the wind from coming in under the doors or sills. Use these anywhere that drafts give you a chill.

A furnace check will ensure that all will fire up ok. A clean filter and a newly serviced unit will be far more efficient than one that needs checking. This is also inexpensive and insures a safe, warm season. You may also want to have your airducts cleaned. This removes debris as well as allergens that can be carried throughout the house. In addition, a chimney sweep can come and service your fireplace to make possible some great cozy nights in front of the fire.

Make sure that your garage doors seat well on the ground when closed. You may need to put some rubber stripping on the bottom to seal any open spots. You can also use storm windows and doors to greatly improve keeping the cold outside. Cover your attic vents to keep cold from entering the roof area and if the temp falls below freezing, let your faucets drip. If you have a propane tank for heating or cooking or water heaters, make sure to have it filled.

Last, if you are going to use space heaters, make sure they are in properly vented areas and away from furniture and curtains as fire may be caused. Electric heaters are my recommendation because there are no harmful fumes to deal with. Well, I hope these tips will make your inter better, warmer and less expensive.

All on USB Credit Card Flash Drive!

iPad Ready!
Tablet Ready!
Smart Phone Ready!

Forms Galore!
40 hours How To Videos

Pete Goes Green!

INCLUDED IN THE SWAT SYSTEM:

40 Hours of Short How To Videos
From basements to the top of the chimney. Short, to the point, how to videos sorted by topic.

Repairs Cost Analyzer Forms
NEVER guess again on knowing what your rehab and repair cost will be.

Job Pricing Software w/Price List
No More Guesstimates - Get Quote

BONUS - Certified Mold Tester
($1,497) includes strategies to maximize your profits when buying.

**BONUS - Tax Free
Profit & Income for LIFE!**
($1,497) includes 6 training videos, a full day workshop, case studies, health savings account, education accounts and more!

PETEYOUNGS@GMAIL.COM ▪ PETEYOUNGS.COM
OFFICE PHONE 404-932-2902 ▪ FAX 770-565-0973

HAVE PETE YOUNGS AT YOUR LOCAL
REIA OR CONVENTION

✓ HOW TO REHAB HOUSES FOR 50% OFF REGULAR CONTRACTOR RATES

✓ EPA MOLD CLASSES WITH CERTIFICATE. GET 25% OFF BANK LISTED REO'S

✓ SIGNATURE HOME DEPOT TOURS AND HOMERS' INVESTOR TOOL TRAINING

✓ HOW AND WHERE TO GET WORKERS FOR UP TO HALF OFF NORMAL RATES

✓ WHERE AND HOW TO GET CONTRACTOR DISCOUNTS OF 40% AND MORE

PETEYOUNGS@GMAIL.COM ▪ PETEYOUNGS.COM
OFFICE PHONE 404-932-2902 ▪ FAX 770-565-0973

RECOMMENDED RESOURCES

TONYYOUNGS.COM

THE HIDDEN MARKET/ONE ON ONE TRAINING

CAMAPLAN.COM

SELF DIRECTED IRA/401K TAX FREE/DIFFERED INVESTING

MIKEBUTLER.COM

QUICKBOOKS FOR REAL ESTATE/LANDLORD EDUCATION

LARRYGOINS.COM

REAL ESTATE CONSULTING/FUNDING/BRAGG RADIO

NATIONALREIA.ORG

NATIONAL GROUPS/R.E. CRUISES/EDUCATION/BENEFITS